*Such Friends*

*1921*

# THE LITERARY 1920s

*"...and say my glory was I had such friends."* —W. B. Yeats

## KATHLEEN DIXON DONNELLY

*"Such Friends": The Literary 1920s, Vol. II—1921*
©2021 by Kathleen Dixon Donnelly

Published by K. Donnelly Communications, Pittsburgh, PA, USA
Printed in the United States of America

ISBN (paperback): 978-1-7364831-2-1

ISBN (eBook): 978-1-7364831-3-8

Other books by Kathleen Dixon Donnelly, available on Amazon

*"Such Friends": The Literary 1920s, Vol. I—1920*

*Manager as Muse: Maxwell Perkins' Work with F. Scott Fitzgerald, Ernest Hemingway and Thomas Wolfe*

*Gypsy Teacher*, a book of blogs chronicling the author's voyages sailing on Semester at Sea and relocating to the United Kingdom

Cover and interior designed by Lisa Thomson, LisaT2@comcast.net

*Cover photo is* A Conversation *by Vanessa Bell, 1913-1916*

*To Tony, Gerty and Bob*

*My new "such friends"*

*"Think where man's glory most begins and ends,*
*and say my glory was I had such friends."*

—The Municipal Gallery Revisited,
William Butler Yeats

# PREFACE

In America, the decade is called The Roaring Twenties; in France, *Les Annees Foules* [The Crazy Years]. In England it is defined by the Bohemian socialites known as the Bright Young Things. But in Ireland the Irish were fighting with the British in their War of Independence and then with each other in the Civil War that followed.

By 1921, the year that this book chronicles, a new American president is coming into office, the Brits are becoming aware of the exciting new art and writing in Europe, while they work with the Irish on a treaty to end their War.

And everyone is coming to Paris.

New American writers—**Gertrude Stein, Dorothy Parker**—are becoming more well-known, not only by publishers in their home country but also by their fellow ex-patriates, founders of the "little mags" hanging out in the Paris cafes. In England, already successful writers such as **Virginia Woolf** are experimenting with new forms. And in Ireland established poets and playwrights, such as **William Butler Yeats**, are becoming more political.

My research for my Ph.D. in Communications from Dublin City University in Ireland focused on the relationships among these creative people who socialized in four writers' salons:

- **Yeats** and the Irish Literary Renaissance,
- **Woolf** and the Bloomsbury Group,
- **Stein** and the Americans in Paris, and
- **Parker** and the Algonquin Round Table.

The first two groups got together before the Great War (1914-1918) but remained friends and active in their creative fields well into the 1920s. The Algonquin Round Table started lunching when many of them came back from the War, in the summer of 1919. I date the beginning of **Gertrude Stein's** group as the summer of 1921 when the Americans came to Paris and sought her out.

The list of the writers and artists I included in each group in my original research follows this preface, and their names appear in boldface throughout the book.

The title for all the work I have done with these creative people is "Such Friends," from Yeats' poetic line, "...and say my glory was I had such friends."

In the 1920s, these creative people had relationships with lots of other interesting "such friends" also. So my research has expanded to include many artists, writers and supporters of the arts who orbited around the original key players. A discussion of the literary life of the early 20th century is not complete without T. S. Eliot, E. M. Forster, James Joyce, D. H. Lawrence or Edna St. Vincent Millay, for example, although none was really a part of any salon.

These incredibly talented friends led mostly normal lives. While they were reinventing art and literature they drank and ate and argued and hung out together.

As 2020 approached, I realized there were going to be a lot of centenaries coming up, and I decided to chronicle the 10 years with blog postings at www.suchfriends.wordpress.com, and gather them in to a series of books. Volume I covering 1920 is available on Amazon in both print and e-book formats, along with this book, Volume II—1921.

Eight more to go!

You can dip in and out of the 100 vignettes in *"Such Friends": The Literary 1920s* series, search to see if your birthday is included, look for mentions of your favorite writers, or read it all straight through from January 1st to December 31st.

Let's find out what these friends were doing in 1921…

# Complete List of "Such Friends"

**The Irish Literary Renaissance** (1897-1906)

William Butler Yeats, poet, playwright
Lady Augusta Gregory, playwright
George Moore, novelist, playwright
AE (George Russell), artist, poet, playwright
Edward Martyn, playwright, philanthropist
John Millington Synge, playwright
Douglas Hyde, playwright, translator, politician

**The Bloomsbury Group** (1907-1915)

Virginia Woolf, novelist, essayist
Vanessa Bell, painter, illustrator
Lytton Strachey, essayist, biographer, critic
Duncan Grant, painter
Leonard Woolf, editor, critic, publisher, political writer
Clive Bell, art critic, essayist
Roger Fry, art critic, painter
John Maynard Keynes, economist, essayist

**The Americans in Paris** (1921-1930)

Gertrude Stein, novelist, essayist, librettist
Alice B. Toklas, cook, publisher, writer
Ernest Hemingway, short story writer, novelist
F. Scott Fitzgerald, novelist, short story writer
Robert McAlmon, poet, novelist, publisher
Virgil Thomson, music critic, composer
Sherwood Anderson, novelist, short story writer
Man Ray, photographer, painter

**The Algonquin Round Table** (1919-1928)

Dorothy Parker, essayist, short story writer, poet, critic
Robert Benchley, humorist, critic, actor
Alexander Woollcott, critic, broadcaster, actor
Marc Connelly, playwright, actor
Harold Ross, reporter, editor
George S Kaufman, playwright, director
FPA (Franklin P. Adams), columnist, critic, broadcaster
Heywood Broun, columnist, sports writer, union organizer

# ACKNOWLEDGEMENTS

Writing is a solitary occupation. But producing a finished work requires a full circle of support. Which I am so lucky to have.

Special thanks, again, to my husband and partner, Tony Dixon. [Willie Yeats was a great companion for most of this process, but now that he has gone on to meet up with his sister, Lady Augusta Gregory, we are thankful to be breaking in Gerty Stein and Bob Benchley.]

As the pandemic came and went, and then came back, our friends Liz and Kevin Tafel-Hurley again came through whenever called on.

To double check some specific information, I have received special help on legal issues from Linda Tashbook once again; on the inaugural European tour of the Harvard Glee Club from Kerry Marsteller and her colleagues at the Harvard University Archives; on the Algonquin Round Table from David Trumbull of the Robert Benchley Society; on James Joyce by Glenn Johnston, @JohnstonGlenn; and on French translations from Nicole Harper.

The beautiful design from Lisa Thomson and the production expertise of Loral Pepoon, co-owner of Selah Press Publishing, were so professional and creative the first time around, we did it all again!

The lists at the end of the book, To Read, To Watch, and To Visit, include most of the excellent sources I relied on for the facts.

My rule of not posting anything on the blog unless someone else reads it has saved me a lot of embarrassment, so I am particularly grateful to my other readers, listed on the next page.

I couldn't have done it without you…

Julian Asenjo
Staci Backauskas
Alex Bassil
Jane E. Beckwith
Melanie Bond
Clarence Curry
Faye Davies
Jim Doan
Patrick J. Donnelly
Helen Fallon
Gregory Grefenstette
Nicole Harper
Marie Hooper
David Hope
Mary Lou Irish
Jonathan Ivy
Glenn Johnston
Maura Judges
Jane Kanga
Hedda Kopf
Ian Marchant

Alyce Marshall
Phil Mason
Jim Monteleone
Robert O'Gara
Anton Perreau
Simon Powell
Janet Purtell
Scott Rossi
Kate Rudy
Ruth Ryals
Elizabeth Ryan
Richard Paul Skinner
Susan Snyder Sponar
Liz Tafel-Hurley
Linda Tashbook
David Trumbull
Eva Tumiel-Kozak
Niki Valentine
Gaby Walter
Neil Weatherall

# ❧ DECEMBER 31, 1920/ ❧
# JANUARY 1, 1921
## IRELAND, ENGLAND, FRANCE AND AMERICA

W hat a year. **F. Scott Fitzgerald's** predicted "greatest, gaudiest spree in history" hasn't materialized—yet.

At the end of the first year of the new decade…

In Ireland, poet and playwright **William Butler Yeats**, 55, and his wife Georgie, 28, are at home, still resting up after an extensive and successful American lecture tour. They are pleased to be back with their daughter, Anne, almost two, and **Yeats** is continuing to work on his autobiography. He has finally admitted to himself that his father, painter John Butler "JB" Yeats, 81, is never going to leave the comfortable life he has in New York City to come back to Ireland.

*Parade in Dublin*

In England, novelist **Virginia Woolf**, 38, and her husband, **Leonard**, 40, are spending the holidays at their East Sussex home, Monk's House near Rodmell. Their almost four-year old publishing company, the Hogarth Press, has lost one of its authors, Katherine Mansfield, 31, to a more established publisher because they had neglected to contract her for more than one book.

*The original Hogarth printing press*

Their latest assistant, Ralph Partridge, 26, has only earned £56 as his share of the company yearly profits. But they have printed and published four titles—including **Virginia's** story, *Kew Gardens,* which has sold 620 copies—and earned £68, 19 shillings, 4 pence.

*1920 Ford touring car*

In France, American ex-patriate writer **Gertrude Stein**, 46, and her partner, **Alice B. Toklas**, 43, recently welcomed a new member of their household on the Left Bank of Paris—Godiva, their new Ford touring car. Their previous auto, "Auntie Pauline," which took them all over France as they volunteered for the Fund for French Wounded during the Great War, finally died right in front of the Luxembourg Palace, the 17th century main government building. The replacement arrived and **Alice** remarked that it was naked—no clock, no cigarette lighter, no ashtray. So **Gertrude** promptly named her Godiva.

❧❧

In America, New York free-lance writer **Dorothy Parker**, 27, is floating. She's getting plenty of her articles and poetry published in magazines, and lunching most days with her fellow writers at the midtown Manhattan Algonquin Hotel. Two of her lunchmates and former *Vanity Fair*

*The Algonquin Hotel*

colleagues, **Robert Benchley**, 31, and Robert Sherwood, 24, are willing to accept silly pieces she submits to their monthly humor magazine, *Life,* and the *Saturday Evening Post* is willing to buy the same kind of fluff. **Dottie** knows that it is not her best work. But it pays the bills.

What will the new year bring?

# ❧ JANUARY 5, 1921 ❧
## TIMES SQUARE, NEW YORK CITY, NEW YORK

Wednesday, January 5th, 6:59 pm. Traffic on Broadway and 7th Avenue whizzes through Times Square, north and south, as it has for decades.

*Times Square*

Wednesday, January 5th, 7:00 pm. Traffic on Broadway and 7th Avenue whizzes through Times Square, northbound only until midnight, while the Broadway shows are entertaining audiences and some critics.

Theatre goers rushing to see the just opened *Diff'rent* by Eugene O'Neill, 32, and 40,000 automobiles manage to not have an accident.

# ❧ MID-JANUARY, 1921 ❧
## DUNDRUM, DUBLIN; AND OXFORD, ENGLAND

Lolly Yeats, 52, owner and business manager of Cuala Press, run out of her home in Dundrum, is still intrigued by some things she observed on a recent visit to the Oxford home of her brother, Irish poet and playwright **William Butler Yeats**, 55, his wife, Georgie, 28, and their daughter Anne, almost two.

She knows **Willie** is proud of his English home, so she didn't say anything. But all of their plates are a dark color, with no pattern. And, odder still, because the couple doesn't own or like silverplate, their cutlery is made out of horn?!

Lolly wrote to her father, painter John Butler "JB" Yeats, 81, living in New York City, asking if he ever had to drink soup from a flat spoon?! Or use a fork with only a couple of prongs to eat a piece of meat?!

However, she did appreciate Georgie's attempts to brighten up their place with brightly colored cushions, and the nice touch of putting both note cards and stamps in each guest's room.

The **Yeatses** seem to be doing well, having just returned from a successful lecture tour of the States last year. But Lolly feels that the check she will be sending **Willie** for his royalties from his Cuala Press publications—which should be almost £500—will be greatly appreciated.

❧❧

In the **Yeatses'** home in Oxford, Georgie is looking forward to their upcoming trip around the south of England, including revisiting Stone Cottage in Sussex where they spent their honeymoon almost four years ago. But recently she has been feeling sick in the mornings, and thinks she had better tell **Willie** that she might be pregnant again. She knows he has been hoping for a boy.

# ❧ JANUARY **15, 1921** ❧
## DAHNTAHN PITTSBURGH, PENNSYLVANIA

Herbert Hoover, 46, will soon become Secretary of Commerce in the incoming administration of President Warren G. Harding, 55. He had the responsibilities of an administer of food supplies during the Great War. But his concern right now is the technology.

*Duquesne Club, Forbes Avenue, Pittsburgh*

Hoover is at Pittsburgh's posh, private Duquesne Club, about to do a live broadcast which will be transmitted along a telephone line 10 miles to the two-month old first radio station in the country, KDKA, which will then broadcast it nationally.

They did successfully broadcast a church service for the first time a couple of weeks ago. But Hoover is more worried about the technology than his speech, which is about the administration's plan for humanitarian relief for postwar Europe.

# ❧ JANUARY, 1921 ❧
## BROADWAY, NEW YORK CITY, NEW YORK

**M**arc Connelly, 30, budding playwright from western Pennsylvania, is pleased with how his Broadway debut play, *Erminie,* is going.

Connelly came east to New York City from his hometown of McKeesport, just south of Pittsburgh, Pennsylvania, about six years ago, working on a play that had been a big hit back home. But it flopped in New York.

Made sense to stay.

Producer George Tyler, 53, asked him to adapt this 19th century comedy opera, *Erminie,* which has been brought back to life many times in the UK and the US.

Erminie

Connelly is thrilled to have the opportunity to work with Tyler. The cigar smoking, gambling producer from Ohio has built his company by bringing European talent to America, including four tours of Dublin's Abbey Theatre with their founder and director **Lady Augusta Gregory**, now 68.

Tyler also produced *Someone in the House* by another western Pennsylvania playwright, **George S Kaufman**, 31, at the end of the Great War. That play didn't do so well, only partially because authorities were telling everyone to stay home to protect themselves from the influenza that was roaring through the city. **Kaufman** paid for ads that said,

❝   Avoid the Crowds!

Come See *Someone in the House*!"

Didn't help.

**Connelly's** *Erminie* is in its third week and **Kaufman** gave it a good review in the *New York Times* where he is an assistant to the main drama critic, **Alexander Woollcott**, about to turn 34.

*George S Kaufman*

**Connelly** and **Kaufman** met a few years ago and have started collaborating and hanging out in the *Times* newsroom, waiting for **Woollcott** to leave so they can use his typewriter. They are working on a play based on a character, *Dulcy,* created by one of the other writers they lunch with regularly at the nearby Algonquin Hotel, **Franklin P. Adams**, 39, better known as the dean of New York columnists, **FPA**.

*Dulcy,* their first joint project, is due to open in Chicago next month; **FPA** has been promised 10% of the profits. If there are any.

# ❦ JANUARY 21, 1921 ❦
## 13 NASSAU STREET, NEW YORK CITY, NEW YORK

John Quinn, 50, corporate lawyer and passionate supporter of the arts, is fed up.

He doesn't mind being busy. But this is ridiculous.

Quinn is trying to serve his corporate, fee-paying clients, but his most important staff member has been hospitalized with diabetes. Of course, Quinn paid the hospital bill and told the clerk to take time off for a trip out to the country. But they really need him back in the office.

The requests he is getting from his creative friends and former lovers are what really has him raving.

The Irish poet and artist **AE [George Russell]**, 53, has been giving him advice on how to approach his defence of *The Little Review* magazine on obscenity charges for serializing sections of the novel *Ulysses,* by Irish writer James Joyce, 38.

In the preliminary hearing last fall, Magistrate Joseph E. Corrigan, 45, an old friend of Quinn's, ruled that the section of *Ulysses,* where, as Quinn describes it, "the man went off in his pants," is definitely "smutty, filthy within the meaning of the statute." So he has scheduled the trial for next month.

And Joyce—he's the most annoying of all. He's writing Quinn from Paris that he MUST have a royalty of $3 or $3.50 per copy if Quinn arranges to have a private edition of *Ulysses* printed. And Joyce refuses to allow the publisher to change even one word.

And then he cables begging for money, which Quinn assumes is to pay for the *Ulysses* manuscript he is buying as Joyce writes it. So he will send the money.

Then Quinn gets a letter from **Lady Augusta Gregory**, 68, his friend and former lover, who wants the names of magazines and estate agents in New

York to help her rent out her home, Coole Park outside of Galway, Ireland. Oh. And could he send some apples? Bad year for apples in Ireland.

American ex-patriate poet, Ezra Pound, 35, his original connection with Joyce, writes from Paris that he wants Quinn to pass on a message to a Japanese Noh actor that he knows. Oh. And could he get him a job as foreign editor for *Century* magazine?

*Previous issue of* Blast

Pound's friend, English writer and painter Wyndham Lewis, 38, writes asking Quinn to get subscribers for his magazine, *Blast,* which he is planning to revive. Oh. And could he buy some more of his paintings? Lewis needs the money.

Former Irish MP Horace Plunkett, 66, writes from Dublin asking Quinn to find some obscure pamphlet so he can get some quotes out of it.

That does it. Quinn figures the one person he can vent to is Pound. He is writing a ranting 10-page letter to him, mentioning that he doesn't have any time to write letters:

❝ I haven't had time to read a book in weeks or to see any art or read about art stuff…I have tried to let you know how busy I am, how driven I am, how harassed I am, but it does not seem to penetrate… Plunkett wrote as though I had a special alcove in my library thoroughly digested and thoroughly classified and all arranged so that all I needed to do would be to step up to [the pamphlet] and tip the thing out with one of my fingers and send it to him. I exist only to supply Plunkett with pamphlets…Good God Almighty, what do they take me for?…I am supposed to work on [Joyce's] contract, advise about the contract, to negotiate it, to make the contract legally possible with this action, and yet at the same time to advance him money. And I suppose I will end by doing it. But, by God, there is an end of him too. I am not the father of his children…Nine times out of 10 these requests are so small that it seems easier to do the God damned infernal things than to refuse them and explain about it…[*The Little Review/Ulysses* trial] will be a miraculous victory if I bring it about."

What Quinn would really rather do is to see the play by the late Oscar Wilde, *The Importance of Being Earnest,* which just opened last night on Broadway.

But first, he's going to write a telegram to Joyce insisting that the Irishman stop cabling him about *anything*. Quinn will tell him that he has been trying to make Joyce and Pound "understand I am working limits of my endurance."

# ❧ JANUARY, 1921 ❧
## 100 EAST CHICAGO STREET, CHICAGO, ILLINOIS

Would-be novelist **Ernest Hemingway**, 21, currently working as editor of a house organ, has been hanging out here at "the Domicile" with a friend, Y. Kenley Smith, 33, who works at the Critchfield Advertising Agency. Smith has brought around one of the other Critchfield copywriters, **Sherwood Anderson**, 44, to meet **Ernest**.

**Hemingway** likes **Anderson**, and he's pleasantly surprised that the feeling is mutual. But his girlfriend, Hadley Richardson, 29, whom he regularly writes to in St. Louis, isn't surprised at all.

❝ Of course he likes you!" she said.

*Sherwood Anderson*

**Anderson**, a bit older and a lot more experienced as a writer, has had short stories published in national magazines and just had a big success last year with his third book, *Winesburg, Ohio*, a collection of related stories about the residents of one town.

The young writer feels that he's been learning a lot from the older novelist. He introduced him to magazines such as *The Dial, American Mercury, Poetry,* and is turning **Ernie** on to contemporary writers such as Floyd Dell, 33, Waldo Frank, 31, Van Wyck Brooks, 35. All real *American*

writers. Through **Sherwood**, **Ernest** even met the Chicago poet Carl Sandburg, 43, who won a special Pulitzer Prize two years ago.

**Anderson** advised **Hemingway** to set aside a room just for writing, as **Sherwood** has done. **Ernest** is learning how to become a writer.

**Anderson** is tired of writing ad copy for tractors and hopes to soon be able to make a living as a full-time fiction writer. This summer, a benefactor has offered to finance his first trip to Europe. **Sherwood** has to find the money to bring along his wife, Tennessee, 46.

*Carl Sandburg*

# ❧ JANUARY, 1921 ❧
## HOTEL DES SAINTS-PERES,
## 65 RUE DES SAINTS PERES, PARIS

Poet Edna St. Vincent Millay, 28, has just arrived at her hotel in Paris. She will be staying here a few months as the newly appointed foreign correspondent for American *Vanity Fair* magazine.

The time had come to leave New York. She is tired of her persistent beau, Edmund "Bunny" Wilson, 25, managing editor of *Vanity Fair,* who not only published her poems but also promoted her as "the Most Distinguished American Poet of the Younger Generation."

This past year, Vincent, as her family knows her, won a few prizes, scored a big hit with her poetry collection, but also had an abortion. She definitely needs a change and is looking forward to starting this great job. Her contract requires her to submit two prose pieces to *Vanity Fair* each month.

Just before she left New York, Vincent received a letter from her father, whom her mother kicked out over 20 years ago. Dad heard about her new job and wrote to give his estranged daughter his idea of encouragement. He knew she would be "a great success at work of that kind [but it is] a big undertaking for such a little girl."

*Hotel des Saints-Peres*

Gee thanks, Dad.

# ❧ FEBRUARY 4, 1921 ❧
## 23 RUE LA BOETIE, RIGHT BANK; AND
## 27 RUE DE FLEURUS, LEFT BANK, PARIS

S panish painter Pablo Picasso, 39, and his wife, Russian-Ukrainian ballerina Olga Khokhlova Picasso, 29, are pleased to welcome their first child, Paulo, born today.

Across the city, at 27 rue de Fleurus, American ex-pat writer **Gertrude Stein**, just turned 47, and her partner, **Alice B. Toklas**, 43, are also pleased. The friendship between **Stein** and Picasso has had its ups and downs recently, but **Gertrude** feels a connection with Paulo because he is born one day after her own birthday. She decides to write him a birthday book, with one line for every day in the year.

# ❧ FEBRUARY, 1921 ❧
## HOTEL MAJESTIC, CENTRAL PARK WEST, NEW YORK CITY, NEW YORK

She's bored. Maybe more than bored. Freelance journalist and fiction writer, Edna Ferber, 35, has her novel *The Girls* coming out later this year, and she shares this great apartment with her Mom. But sometimes, particularly when her mother is out with friends, Edna wants to go out and play. And sometimes there is no one to play with.

*Alexander Woollcott*

Her favorite theatre companion these days is *New York Times* drama critic **Alexander Woollcott**, 34. Edna loves the glamor of opening nights; **Aleck** always has tickets and likes to wear his opera hat and cape.

But, after a terrific night in the theatre, instead of moving on to a speakeasy for a late night drink, **Alex** dumps Edna into a taxi and races to his *Times* office to write his review.

Last week Ferber had gone on a shopping spree and when she came home, she felt like having a companion for a candlelit dinner. She'd called **Alex** and sent him a note, but he didn't bother to answer.

Edna likes having a male friend to squire her around town, and **Alex** feels safe to her.

But annoying. She teases him about his deplorably unhealthy eating habits—gooey desserts and coffee all day—and he has also more than once ruined her dinner parties by arriving up to an hour late.

Ferber plans to ask **Woollcott** to take her to lunch some day soon with his friends at the Algonquin Hotel. All writers and artists on the city's magazines and newspapers, they are the type of people Edna would love to get to know.

# ❧ FEBRUARY **14, 1921** ❧
## NEW YORK CITY, NEW YORK

Margaret Anderson, 34, founder and publisher of the literary magazine *The Little Review,* is disappointed. As is her partner, the magazine's editor, Jane Heap, 37.

They are not happy about being served with papers last year for publishing "obscene" excerpts from *Ulysses,* the latest work in progress by Irish novelist James Joyce, just turned 39. And they are grateful that their lawyer, art collector John Quinn, 50, is not charging them a fee for all the work he has been doing.

But here they are in the New York City Court of Special Sessions and Quinn's main argument is that no one would understand *Ulysses* anyway, so how can it be obscene?!

Quinn started off alright by presenting Joyce's reputation as a respected man of letters, but when one of the judges asked how that was relevant, Quinn dropped it. He put a few well-known writers on the stand, but they just testified that the novel wouldn't corrupt readers.

Anderson calls *Ulysses* "the prose masterpiece of my generation." She and Heap want the defense to be that it is great literature and should not be suppressed.

Quinn will have none of that. He already told Anderson that the case is unwinnable and he has no intention of appealing a guilty verdict. And he doesn't think they should have published such material in a magazine anyway, because it is sent through the mails. Quinn has been trying to convince Joyce to agree to a privately published book, which couldn't possibly be prosecuted.

Playing to the three-judge panel, Quinn seizes on the anger of the lead prosecutor:

66 There is my best exhibit. There is proof that *Ulysses* does not corrupt or fill people full of lascivious thoughts. Look at him! He is mad all over. He wants to hit somebody. He doesn't want to love anybody. He wants somebody to be punished. He's mad. He's angry. His face is distorted with anger, not with love. That's what Joyce does. That's what *Ulysses* does. It makes people angry. They want to break something. They want somebody to be convicted. They feel like prosecuting everybody connected with it, even if they don't know how to pronounce the name *Ulysses*. But it doesn't tend to drive them to the arms of some siren."

Anderson feels that the whole scene is surreal. When the prosecutor is about to read out one of the main offending passages from *Ulysses'* "Nausicaa" section, one of the judges actually says that Anderson (ignoring Heap) should be excused from the room as she is a young woman. Quinn points out that she is the one who published that passage. The judge says that she can't possibly understand the significance of what she is publishing.

Oh, yes I do, thinks Margaret.

Court is recessed for one week so the judges can read the full "Nausicaa" episode.

※◦※

In another New York City courtroom, American self-published poet and general drifter **Robert McAlmon**, 25, is marrying English writer Annie Winifred Ellerman, 26, known by her adopted name, Bryher.

*Newlyweds Bryher and Robert McAlmon*

The couple met through friends at a Greenwich Village party just recently. Bryher explained to **McAlmon** that she is from a very well-to-do British family. But they are holding on to her rightful inheritance until she gets married.

So, if they get married, they can take the money and move to Paris! **McAlmon** figures this sounds like a pretty good deal.

# ❧ MID-FEBRUARY, 1921 ❧
## MANHATTAN, NEW YORK CITY, NEW YORK

E dmund Wilson, 25, managing editor of *Vanity Fair,* was pleased when his friend from his Princeton University years, **F. Scott Fitzgerald**, 24, asked him to edit a draft of his second novel, *The Flight of the Rocket.*

> TO
>
> SHANE LESLIE, GEORGE JEAN NATHAN
>
> AND MAXWELL PERKINS
>
> IN APPRECIATION OF MUCH LITERARY HELP
>
> AND ENCOURAGEMENT

*Dedication page of Fitzgerald's second novel*

At first Wilson felt that the story is a bit silly, just a re-hashing of **Fitzgerald's** dramatic summer spent fighting with his new wife, Zelda, 20, in Westport, Connecticut.

But now that he has gotten farther into the manuscript, Wilson is beginning to see that **Fitzgerald's** writing has matured and shows more emotional power than his previous fiction. Might want to change that title, though.

Earlier this month, **Fitzgerald** wrote to his Scribner's editor, Maxwell Perkins, 36, to assure him that he is "working like the deuce" on the novel, whose publication date has been postponed a few times already.

**Fitzgerald** also mentioned that his income taxes are due and he's about $1,000 short, signing the letter "Inevitable Beggar."

Perkins writes back to assure him that he is still owed a couple of thousand dollars in royalties from his hit first novel, *This Side of Paradise.*

# ❧ FEBRUARY 21, 1921 ❧
## COURT OF SPECIAL SESSIONS, NEW YORK CITY, NEW YORK; AND LEFT BANK, PARIS

*The Little Review's* founder and publisher, Margaret Anderson, 34, and editor, Jane Heap, 37, are back in court with their pro bono lawyer, John Quinn, 50, to hear the verdict of the three-judge panel in their trial for publishing in their magazine allegedly "obscene" excerpts from *Ulysses,* the work in progress of Irish novelist James Joyce, 39, currently living in Paris.

The judges have spent the week since the trial reading the whole "Nausicaa" episode which was published in three issues of *The Little Review* last year.

Guilty.

Pay a $100 fine and don't publish any more episodes of *Ulysses.* End of.

❧❧❧

In Paris, French poet Valery Larbaud, 39, has been reading the sections of *Ulysses* in *The Little Review* which his friend, American ex-patriate

bookseller Sylvia Beach, 33, has recommended to him. He can't believe it. Joyce is a genius. Every bit as great as Rabelais. Larbaud hasn't been this excited by an author since he first read Walt Whitman as a teenager. He has to write to Sylvia and ask: Maybe Mr. Joyce will allow him to translate some segments into French?!

*The Little Review*

# ✂ FEBRUARY 26, 1921 ✄

## ABBEY THEATRE, 26/27 ABBEY STREET LOWER;
## AND ST. STEPHEN'S GREEN, DUBLIN

Irish poet, playwright and Abbey Theatre co-founder **William Butler Yeats**, 55, is hoping that this production will bring in additional audience members who are moved by stories of the heroes of the ongoing Irish rebellion against British rule.

*Terence MacSwiney*

*The Revolutionist* is the most overtly political play that **Yeats** and his co-founder and theatre director, **Lady Augusta Gregory**, 68, have put on at the Abbey. Its author, former Lord Mayor of Cork, the late Terence MacSwiney, is considered a martyr for Ireland since his death last October, after 74 days of hunger strike in the British Brixton Prison.

**Yeats** is sure that his countrymen will recognize MacSwiney in the character of the play's hero.

The Abbey premiered *The Revolutionist* just two days ago, and today is the first Saturday matinee. It's been a success and is repeating next weekend.

One of the actors, Barry Fitzgerald, 32, has been a big hit at the Abbey the past few years, while continuing to work full-time as a government civil servant.

**Yeats** thinks that the play is pretty light on plot and structure but very poetic. He is thinking of repeating *The Revolutionist* in the fall, following it up with a new version of his own *The King's Threshold,* which deals with a hunger strike.

Across the River Liffey, in St. Stephen's
Green, revolutionary Maud Gonne, 54, **Yeats'**
former lover, is writing to their mutual New
York friend, attorney and supporter of the arts
John Quinn, 50:

*Maud Gonne*

❝  My dear Friend

...Here we are having a very strenuous
and trying time, but the heroism and
courage of everyone makes one proud
of being Irish. The English may batter us to pieces but they will never
succeed in breaking our spirit...[her daughter] Iseult (Mrs. Stuart)...
is staying with me. Her baby will be born next month. Luckily her
nerves are pretty good, for Dublin is a terrible place just now. Hardly
a night passes that one is not woke up by the sound of firing. Often
there are people killed, but often it is only the crown forces firing to
keep up their courage. One night last week there was such a terrible
fusillade just outside our house, that we all got up thinking something
terrible was happening. That morning, when curfew regulations
permitted us to go out, we only found the bodies of a cat and dog
riddled with bullets."

Gonne also asks Quinn if he can find an agent for her, as she would like
to have her political articles printed in American publications. She needs
the money.

# ❧ MARCH 4, 1921 ❧
## UNITED STATES CAPITOL, WASHINGTON, D.C.

Ohioan Warren G. Harding, 55, is standing on the East Portico of the Capitol Building, waiting to take the oath of office to become the first sitting Senator and the first Baptist to be inaugurated President of the United States.

Given the state of the nation's economy, at his request the whole day will be relatively quiet. No parade. No inaugural ball.

However, at the insistence of his wife, Florence, 60, Harding is planning to announce that this week the White House will be open to the public for the first time since the start of the Great War. It's time for his promised "Return to Normalcy."

In keeping with tradition, his predecessor, President Woodrow Wilson, 64, has invited the Hardings to a small luncheon at the White House after the swearing in ceremony. Harding, a Republican, has greatly appreciated the professional courtesy Wilson, a Democrat, has shown during this peaceful transfer of power, despite Wilson suffering a serious stroke just five months before.

*Inauguration of Warren G. Harding*

But first, Harding is planning to break with tradition by going directly to a special executive session of Congress to personally present his nominees for his Cabinet (all agreed to by Florence), including Andrew W. Mellon, 65, for Secretary of the Treasury and Herbert Hoover, 64, for Secretary of Commerce.

Fingering a printer's ruler that he keeps in his pocket for good luck—leftover from his days on the newspaper back in Marion, Ohio—the president-elect puts his right hand on the George Washington Bible and says,

" I, Warren Gamaliel Harding, do solemnly swear that I will faithfully execute the office of President of the United States, and will, to the best of my ability, preserve, protect and defend the Constitution of the United States."

# ❦ MARCH 8, 1921 ❧
## HOGARTH HOUSE, RICHMOND, LONDON

She's feeling rather pleased with herself. Novelist **Virginia Woolf**, 39, has just brought out her first collection of short stories, published by her and her husband, **Leonard**, 40, at their own four-year-old Hogarth Press.

*Monday or Tuesday* is one of the more ambitious projects they have tackled, having started with individual stories. This is full book length, with some stories that have appeared before and some new.

Monday or Tuesday *with cover by Vanessa Bell*

Her sister, painter **Vanessa Bell**, 41, did a woodcut for the cover, which she has done for many of Hogarth's books. This time they also had **Vanessa** do a few more for the inside pages.

**Virginia** feels that both the writing and the art are up to her high standards.

However.

The printing is a mess.

The **Woolfs** trusted McDermott's Prompt Press, which they have used before, and what they got is what **Virginia** describes to a friend as "an odious object…[which leaves] black stains wherever it touches." And all 1,000 copies are filled with typographical errors.

That problem is no trouble to fix. They'll correct the typos for the Harcourt Brace American edition and never use McDermott again.

The problem she is having trouble fixing is her third novel, *Jacob's Room*. **Virginia** is trying to continue the experiments with style she used in the newer short stories in *Monday or Tuesday*. But working here in the **Woolfs'** house in Richmond, with the business of the Hogarth Press going on all around her—it's just not coming. She likes to write in her head when she walks out on the Sussex countryside surrounding their country home, Monk's House. Earlier this month she wrote in her diary,

❝❝    If I were at Rodmell I should have thought it all out walking on the flats. I should be in writing trim."

This short story collection is giving her confidence. She writes in her diary now,

❝❝    And I'm not nearly as pleased as I was depressed; & yet in a state of security; fate cannot touch me; the reviewers may snap; & sales decrease…[I have overcome my fear of being] dismissed as negligible."

# ✄ MARCH 13, 1921 ✄
## SHILLINGFORD, BERKSHIRE, ENGLAND

Irish poet and playwright **William Butler Yeats**, 55, is writing to his friend and fellow founder of Dublin's Abbey Theatre, **Lady Augusta Gregory**, about to turn 69, back in her home in Coole Park in the west of Ireland.

**Yeats** wants to explain to her why he and his pregnant wife, Georgie, 28, and their two-year-old daughter Anne, have moved from the place they rented in Oxford to this cottage in Berkshire.

Mainly, to save money. Not only is there a baby on the way [**Yeats** is hoping for a boy], but **Willie** is still sending money to New York to support his father, painter John Butler "JB" Yeats, almost 82. Thankfully, Dad is being watched over by their friend, Irish-American lawyer and art collector, John Quinn, 50. Quinn often buys some of **Willie's** manuscripts, giving the money to JB to keep him going.

*Shillingford Bridge, Berkshire*

But **Yeats** and his sisters are pressuring Dad to move back home. To no avail.

The **Yeatses** also considered moving back to Ireland. But their tower in the west of the country, Thoor Ballylee, has been terribly flooded by the recent rains. And living there, near Galway, is too dangerous now with the War of Independence raging.

So **Willie** and Georgie found this cottage in Shillingford, about 10 miles south of Oxford, which will reduce their expenses. And it is within walking distance of the town's Catholic Church. Of course, the **Yeatses** are Protestants. But the proximity makes it more convenient for their maids.

# ❧ SPRING, 1921 ❧
## HOTEL SAINTS-PERES,
## 65 RUE DES SAINTS PERES, PARIS

Back in her hotel room, American poet Edna St. Vincent Millay, 29, foreign correspondent for *Vanity Fair* magazine, has been out all evening at one of the cafes in the nearby Latin Quarter.

Millay really has been enjoying the past few months living in Paris. She quickly became fluent in French, has been invited to parties, and loves the bawdiness of French theatre. The only thing that doesn't agree with her is the dairy-rich diet, particularly the coffee and cream.

But tonight. Tonight.

She'd gone to the café with one of her

*George Slocombe*

on-again, off-again lovers, British journalist Griffin Barry, 37. He introduced her to the most striking man in the room, red-headed, red-bearded English George Slocombe, 27, special correspondent for the *London Daily Herald*. He was wearing a black hat and a striking ascot.

Edna felt the attraction right away. And so did he. She told him about her job and her family back in New York. He talked about the international political stories he has been covering and explained that he had lost two teeth in the Great War.

On the way home in a cheap taxi, Edna could think of nothing but him. They had made plans to meet up tomorrow for a walk in the Bois de Boulogne.

George had left the café before her. He had to get back to his wife and three children in Saint-Cloud.

# ❧ SPRING, 1921 ❧
## MAYFAIR, LONDON

Sitting in his new in-laws' posh house, American publisher, poet, and general drifter **Robert McAlmon**, 26, can't believe his luck.

Back in February he had accepted the offer of a woman he had just met, Annie Ellerman, also 26, always known as Bryher, to get married so she could have access to her family money. Until they came over here to introduce **Bob** to her parents, he hadn't realized how much family money there is.

The *New York Times* broke the story this month that the daughter of Sir John Ellerman, 58, first baronet, owner of British newspapers, breweries and shipping lines and the richest man in the United Kingdom, had married some unknown writer and artists' model, **Robert McAlmon**. The family made no comment.

**McAlmon** is getting along well with his new British in-laws. Bryher's parents have succumbed to his charms and promised him a generous allowance. He even has enjoyed chatting with her younger brother John, 11, a reclusive boy. He writes books about rodents.

The newlyweds had hosted a big party at the Hotel Brevoort before their sailing. His fellow co-founder of *Contact* magazine, poet Dr. William Carlos Williams, 37, had brought the couple orchids. **McAlmon** did explain to him later that it was a marriage of convenience only.

And how convenient it has turned out for **Bob**. Bryher is introducing him to most of the literary lights of London. Writer and painter Wyndham Lewis, 38, has agreed to publish two of **McAlmon's** poems in his magazine, *Blast*. Publisher and philanthropist Harriet Shaw Weaver, 44, will publish some in her magazine, *The Egoist,* and is talking about bringing out a whole collection. American ex-patriate poet T. S. Eliot, 32, has introduced him to Bloomsbury art critic, **Clive Bell**, 39, although Eliot doesn't seem to take **Bell** seriously as a writer.

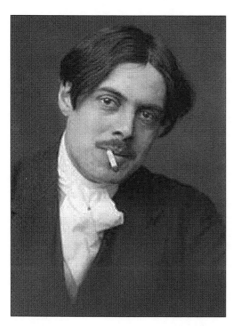

*Wyndham Lewis*

**McAlmon** and Bryher agree that one of the best uses of her money is supporting fledgling writers like themselves. She has given funds to Weaver's Egoist Press to publish new poets. In return, Weaver has given **McAlmon** a letter of introduction to one of his literary idols, Irish novelist James Joyce, 39. He can't wait to look him up as soon as they move to Paris.

# ✥ MARCH, 1921 ✥
## CHARLESTON FARMHOUSE, EAST SUSSEX, ENGLAND

**V**anessa Bell, 41, painting at her country home, Charleston, is pleased to have her work in an exhibit, "Some Contemporary English Artists," on now at the Independent Gallery in Grafton Street in the posh Mayfair section of London.

Also included in the exhibit is work by her partner, **Duncan Grant**, 36.

Last month her brother Adrian Stephen, 37, and his wife Karin, 32, both psychologists, commissioned **Vanessa** and **Duncan** to decorate their rooms at 40 Gordon Square, the same part of Bloomsbury where **Vanessa** has lived since her father died in 1904.

And the two painters are still working on a big commission from their Bloomsbury friend, economist **John Maynard Keynes**, 37, to create new murals for his rooms at King's College, Cambridge. Since last summer they have been producing eight allegorical figures, alternating male and female, to fill almost a whole wall, representing Science, Political Economics, Music, Classics, Law, Mathematics, Philosophy and History as well as advising **Maynard** on every detail of the interior decoration of the sitting room, right down to the color of the curtains.

So they are busy. Together. They work well as a team and have received recognition. But **Vanessa** is worried that her painting is becoming too much like **Duncan's**.

What **Vanessa** really wants is to have a solo exhibit of her own work. As **Duncan** did last year.

*John Maynard Keynes*

# ❧ MARCH 31, 1921 ❧
## SHAKESPEARE AND COMPANY, 8 RUE DUPUYTREN, PARIS

Sylvia Beach, just turned 34, American ex-pat owner of this bookstore, Shakespeare and Company, knows that she has to be the one to bring the bad news.

She has received a clipping of an editorial in last month's *New York Tribune* stating that the court has ruled that excerpts from *Ulysses,* the work in progress by Irish novelist James Joyce, 39, her friend and customer, are officially, legally obscene.

And the "melancholy Jesus," as she calls him, has just walked into her store.

Joyce has been working on this novel for over six years now, and the late nights in a dimly lit room have severely affected his eyesight. He says he is now writing the last two sections and will be finished by May. Sylvia is dubious.

Recently he received a briefcase, sent from his previous home in Trieste, Italy, containing 12-year-old love letters between him and his partner and mother of his children, Nora Barnacle, just turned 37. This will help him to write the ending he has planned.

Despite the efforts of his benefactor in New York, lawyer and art collector John Quinn, 50, to get a major publisher to bring out a private edition, the only place excerpts of *Ulysses* have appeared in the States is in *The Little Review.* And now the magazine's publishers have been fined and prohibited from publishing any more.

After reading the clipping Joyce says,

❝    My book will never come out now."

What disturbs him even more is that, according to the *Tribune* editorial, the defense that Quinn used in court was that the novel was incomprehensible to the average reader and disgusting. But not obscene. Because most people couldn't understand it anyway, what was the point in suppressing it?

The judges didn't agree. And they had recently punished a publisher in another obscenity case with a choice between a $1,000 fine or three months in prison. *The Little Review* publishers take this all seriously.

Sylvia feels for Joyce. His short story collection, *Dubliners,* had been rejected by 22 publishers before being brought out by Grant Richards Ltd. seven years ago in London.

What can she do to help? Does she know any publishers here? Her partner, Adrienne Monnier, 28, who owns a French-language bookshop a few blocks away, has been bringing out *Les Cahiers des Amis des Livres,* a series of French writing and translations, for almost two years now. She works with a printer in Dijon and knows about typesetting and production.

Quinn had talked to Joyce about creating a private, high quality edition to sell for $10. Sylvia is thinking that she could have three different versions, of varying quality, and charge twice that much for a signed limited edition.

If she sets up a subscription scheme to get orders in advance, Sylvia figures she could pay the printer in instalments. And she could also hit up her mother and sisters for more family money to cover upfront expenses.

Sylvia knows little about publishing, but she knows how to sell books. Not only is she fond of Joyce, she loves his work and has read enough of this novel to know that it will be one of the most important works published in English this decade.

Beach turns to Joyce and says,

  ❝  Mr. Joyce, would you let Shakespeare and Company have the honor of bringing out your *Ulysses?*"

# ❧ APRIL, 1921 ❧
## SHILLINGFORD, BERKSHIRE, ENGLAND

Irish poet and playwright **William Butler Yeats**, 55, is thrilled to find out that Iseult Gonne Stuart, 26, whom he thinks of as a daughter, has had her first child.

*Iseult Gonne Stuart*

To be honest, **Yeats** has been in love with Iseult's mother, Irish independence activist, Maud Gonne, 54, since they met over 30 years ago. Many times during their stormy relationship he proposed marriage and she always turned him down. Eventually she even suggested that he propose to Iseult instead. And *she* turned him down.

**Willie** is now happily married to Georgie Hyde-Lees Yeats, 28. They have a daughter, Anne, two, and are expecting another child in August. **Willie** really wants a boy.

**Yeats** has done Iseult the favor of creating a horoscope for her new daughter. He writes to her suggesting that perhaps her Dolores will grow up to marry his expected son! He adds,

❝ By that time I shall be very old and stern & with my authority to support yours, she will do in that matter what she is told to do."

# ❧ APRIL **10, 1921** ❧
## BOULEVARD RASPAIL, PARIS

Irish ex-patriate James Joyce, 39, figures he has to write to his benefactor in London, Harriet Shaw Weaver, 44, founder of the Egoist Press, who has been supportive—financially and morally—of his current novel-in-progress, *Ulysses*.

*Harriet Shaw Weaver*

Just last week Joyce reported to her the distressing results of the trial back in New York that stopped publication of excerpts from his novel in *The Little Review* magazine by declaring that they were obscene. He was so upset, he took the time to transcribe by hand the full article from the *New York Tribune* clipping that he'd been given. He added that he knows 1921 is going to be unlucky because the digits add up to 13.

Now there is even worse news to report.

The English woman currently typing his manuscript showed up here at his hotel the other night. Her husband, an employee at the British embassy, found the manuscript and, when he read it, became furious. He ripped up the papers and threw them into the burning fire, including pages from the original as well as her already typed script.

She came back to Joyce the next day with what she could retrieve.

Joyce realizes that the damage is so great that the only complete copy of the "Circe" section he has been working on for so long is right now on board a steamship to New York City. Joyce has been selling the clean copies to one of his other benefactors, Irish-American attorney John Quinn, 50, to raise money to support himself and his family.

The copies Joyce has been giving to the typists are so sloppy that they are driving the women nuts. This is the ninth typist he has hired—just for the "Circe" chapter.

He knows he has to tell Weaver about this disaster, but Joyce also has some good news to pass on:

66  I arranged for a Paris publication to replace the American one—or rather I accepted a proposal made to me by *Shakespeare and Company,* a bookseller's here...The proposal is to publish here in October an edition (complete) of the book...1,000 copies with 20 copies extra for libraries and press. A prospectus will be sent out next week...They offer me 66% of the net profit...The actual printing will begin as soon as the number of orders covers approximately the cost of printing... [Until the profits arrive] I need an advance."

# ✂ MID-APRIL, 1921 ✂
## GREENWICH VILLAGE, NEW YORK CITY, NEW YORK

Photographer and painter **Man Ray**, 30, is proud of his latest work. He and his friend, French painter and surrealist Marcel Duchamp, 33, have produced the first issue of a magazine, *New York Dada.*

New York Dada, *issue #1*

They put a lot of effort into it, particularly the cover. To the uninitiated, it is a small photo of a perfume bottle, *Belle Helaine, Eau de Voilette,* with a not particularly attractive woman on the label.

But their friends in Greenwich Village will recognize "her" as Rrose Selavy, one of the many pseudonyms Duchamp uses. In French the name sounds like *"Eros, c'est la vie,"* which translates as "Eros, such is life," or even *"arroser la vie"* meaning "to toast to life." Duchamp had the original idea and together they dressed him in a coy hat and makeup for the photo **Ray** took.

The surreal theme continues inside with a picture of one of their surreal friends, artist and writer Baroness Elsa von Freytag-Loringhoven, 46, whose poetry has appeared in *The Little Review* magazine.

Although Dada in the United States has developed separately from its European counterpart, **Ray** and Duchamp have managed to include in the issue a letter from the founder of the European movement, Tristan Tzara, about to turn 25, giving them permission to use the name "Dada" for their magazine. In his letter Tzara says,

*Rrose Selavy*

> " Dada belongs to everybody…like the idea of God or the tooth-brush… [There] is nothing more incomprehensible than Dada. Nothing more indefinable."

# ❧ APRIL **17, 1921** ❧
## HOGARTH HOUSE, RICHMOND, LONDON

Novelist **Virginia Woolf**, 39, is concerned about the sales of her most recent book. Her first short story collection, *Monday or Tuesday*, was published last month by the Hogarth Press, which she owns and operates with her husband **Leonard**, 40.

Today she writes in her diary,

❝ Sales & revenues flag, & I much doubt if *M. & T.* will sell 500, or cover expenses."

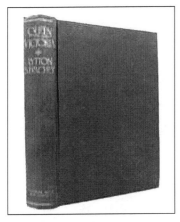

Queen Victoria *by Lytton Strachey*

First, the book looks horrible. Terrible printing job. The **Woolfs** will never use that printer again.

Then their assistant, Ralph Partridge, 27, screwed up the publicity from the start by sending a review copy to the *Times* that didn't include the publication date. All she got was a tiny write-up in an obscure part of the paper.

In the meantime, the new biography, *Queen Victoria* by her friend **Lytton Strachey**, 41, is featured in the paper with three columns of unabashed praise! **Virginia** has also heard that **Lytton's** book sold 5,000 copies in the same week hers only moved 300. No wonder.

**Lytton** dedicated his book to **Virginia**, and he has been complimentary about her collection, particularly the story "The String Quartet."

But the slow sales are beginning to depress **Virginia**. On the other hand, when she receives reports of strong sales she worries that she is becoming too commercial.

A little over a week ago **Virginia** confided to her diary,

❝ I ought to be writing *Jacob's Room*; and I can't, and instead I shall write down the reasons why I can't…Well, you see, I'm a failure as a writer… And thus I can't get on with *Jacob's*…My temper sank and sank till for half an hour I was as depressed as I ever am. I mean I thought of never writing any more—save reviews…What depresses me is the thought that I have ceased to interest people…One does *not* want an established reputation, such as I think I was getting, as one of our leading female novelists. I have still, of course, to gather in all the private criticism, which is the real test."

# ✸ APRIL 21, 1921 ✸
## BOULEVARD RASPAIL, PARIS; AND
## 13 NASSAU STREET, NEW YORK CITY, NEW YORK

In Paris, Irish ex-patriate James Joyce, 39, is writing to one of his benefactors, Irish-American lawyer John Quinn, about to turn 51, in New

442 - PARIS — L'Hôtel Lutétia    A. P.
et le Boulevard Raspail
Lutetia Hotel and Raspail Boulevard

*Boulevard Raspail*

York City, who has been trying to have a publisher bring out a private edition of Joyce's novel-in-progress, *Ulysses*.

Quinn has been supporting Joyce for the past few years, not only by defending the publication of *Ulysses* excerpts in the American

magazine, *The Little Review,* but also by buying up the manuscript for cash as Joyce works on it.

The legal help has been greatly appreciated, but this past February the court ruled that the sections are obscene and stopped their publication.

Now that Sylvia Beach, 34, owner of Paris bookstore Shakespeare and Company, has offered to publish the novel, Joyce feels he needs to pass the news on to Quinn:

❝ The publication of *Ulysses* (complete) was arranged here [in Paris] in a couple of days...Best thanks for your advocacy."

*Horace Liveright*

Back in New York, Quinn has just received the call he has been waiting for from Horace Liveright, 36. His company, Boni and Liveright, is interested in bringing out a private publication of *Ulysses,* which Quinn has been pitching to them for most of the past year. Private publication of a book won't be subject to the same legal restrictions as the magazine, which is sent through the mails.

Quinn's staff tells him that a package has just arrived from Paris containing "Circe," the latest section of Joyce's manuscript.

Eagerly, Quinn begins to read the handwritten pages, and his optimism quickly fades. He realizes that no matter how it is published, this will be a legal disaster. Anyone who would take the chance would be convicted.

He calls Liveright back.

# ❧ END OF APRIL, 1921 ❧
## SCRIBNER'S, 153-157 FIFTH AVENUE, NEW YORK CITY, NEW YORK

F. Scott Fitzgerald, 24, has just brought the manuscript of his latest novel to his editor, Maxwell Perkins, 36, in his office at Charles Scribner's Sons.

**Scott** has been working on this book since last summer when he and his new bride Zelda Sayre Fitzgerald, 20, were living in Westport, Connecticut, supporting the local bootlegger.

Then it was called *The Flight of the Rocket.* He has changed the title to *The Beautiful and Damned.*

*Scribner's*

Perkins is pleased to finally have the manuscript in hand. **Fitzgerald's** first novel, *This Side of Paradise,* was a huge hit for the publisher last year, and Max is proud of his discovery. He had to fight the editorial board to publish **Scott's** story of young people partying after the end of the Great War.

*The Beautiful and Damned* has been an easier sell inside the company.

**Fitzgerald** has only had a few short stories published so far this year. Back in January, Perkins had gotten him $1,600 cash from part of his royalties on the first novel.

Now **Scott** is asking his editor for another $600. He and his pregnant wife want to buy steamship tickets to sail to Europe.

After he leaves the office, Perkins notices that **Fitzgerald** has left behind his copy of his Scribner's contract.

# ❧ SPRING, 1921 ❧
## CHICAGO, ILLINOIS

Would-be novelist **Ernest Hemingway**, 21, is feeling unsure about what direction he is going.

He has a job paying $40 a week editing the *Co-Operative Commonwealth,* a house organ supposedly devoted to spreading the word about the co-operative movement. But **Ernie** is starting to have doubts about the ethics of the publisher, the Co-Operative Society of America, as well as the trustees. He's thinking he could do some investigative digging for the *Chicago Tribune,* even though that would probably cost him this job.

More encouraging is his growing relationship with Hadley Richardson, 29, the lovely redhead whom **Hemingway** met last year at a party.

They've been corresponding almost daily, and **Ernie** has told her about how he was injured in Italy during the Great War. He embellished the truth a bit. And lied about his age.

After **Hemingway** visited the Richardson family in St. Louis, Hadley came to Chicago for a few weeks. She and her chaperone stayed at the posh Plaza Hotel, and **Ernie** took her to meet his parents in nearby Oak Park. His Mom invited them to Sunday dinner—but they forgot to go! Hadley wrote the

*Lobby of Plaza Hotel, Chicago*

Hemingways a lovely apology, but **Ernie** didn't bother to give it to them.

*Ernest Hemingway and Hadley Richardson*

Now that Hadley has gone home, he's been spending his time working on the newsletter, submitting free-lance pieces to the *Toronto Star,* doing lots of reading. And writing Hadley almost every day.

**Hemingway** is thinking that it might be time to leave this job. Even this country. And probably time to marry Hadley.

# ❧ MAY 4, 1921 ❧
## DUNDRUM, DUBLIN

Lily Yeats, 54, co-owner of Cuala Press with her sister, is writing to their father, painter John Butler "JB" Yeats, 82, in New York City.

The family has given up begging him to move back home; Lily is writing to vent her fears about the Irish War of Independence which seems to be raging all around her.

The war started with the Easter Rising over five years ago. Since last year the Black and Tans—unemployed former soldiers from the Great War who have been recruited into the Royal Irish Constabulary, the British occupying force—have been violently marauding throughout the country.

Even in this posh Dublin suburb, three lorries of the thugs came racing down a nearby street the other night. The Yeats' maid had to fall face down on the road to avoid being shot.

At the beginning of the year a British commission published a report strongly criticizing their behavior, and both the British Labour and Liberal parties have lambasted the Conservative government for its policy of violence to the Irish people.

Just this month, Pope Benedict XV, 66, issued a letter urging the "English as well as Irish to calmly consider…some means of mutual agreement." The Brits had thought he was going to condemn the rebellion. Now he's saying that there are bad people on both sides.

A few months ago, Lily's brother, poet and playwright **William Butler Yeats**, 55, now living safely in Berkshire, England, took part in an Oxford debate condemning the British policy. As he does, **Willie** dramatically spoke while striding up and down the aisles of the auditorium. It worked. He won the debate in favor of Irish self-government and against British reprisals.

Lily is writing to her Da,

    " if the present state of affairs goes on, England will have no friends left in Ireland…Some say the Crown forces were *very drunk*— drunk or sober they are ruffians—what will *dear* England do with them when the time comes—it must come sometime that they have to be disbanded?"

*The Black and Tans outside a Dublin hotel*

# ✻ MAY 7, 1921 ✻

## HOTEL DU QUAI VOLTAIRE, 19 QUAI VOLTAIRE, PARIS

As soon as he wakes up, English art critic **Clive Bell**, 39, can't wait to draft a letter to his mistress back in London, writer Mary Hutchinson, 32, about his memorable evening the night before.

**Clive** and some friends started with drinks at Les Deux Magots in Place Saint-Germain des Prés, moving on to dinner at Marchaud's, a few blocks away at rue Jacob and rue des Saints-Peres, where there were bound to be a lot of Americans. The food is good and it's very affordable.

One of **Clive's** friends sees two men he knows in the next room and invites them over to the table. **Clive** tells Mary that he didn't recognize one of the men, but was told he is

    **❝** a bad sort—speaks only about his own books and their value in a French [accent] out of an opera bouffe. And who do you think [he] was? The creature immediately thrust an immense card under my nose and on it was the name of your favorite author—James Joyce. His companion, who happily spoke not one word of French, was called **[Robert] McAlmon**…and gives himself out as the most intimate friend of the well-known American poet—T. S. Eliot. God what a couple. Joyce did not seem stupid, but pretentious, underbred and provincial beyond words: and what an accent. **McAlmon** is an American. They both think nobly of themselves, well of Ezra Pound and poorly of Wyndham Lewis…The little nuisance [who had brought the two over] broke in drunkenly on Joyce's incessant monologue of self-appreciation. [Joyce looks like] exactly what a modern genius ought to be…like something between an American traveller in flash jewellery and a teacher in a Glasgow socialist Sunday school."

**Clive** decides that in his wanderings around Paris he is going to avoid Joyce.

# ❧ EARLY MAY, 1921 ❧
## EN ROUTE FROM NEW YORK CITY TO PARIS

Eleanor Beach, 59, in the middle of the Atlantic Ocean, is enjoying her crossing. She's looking forward to seeing her daughters—she calls them her "chicks"—who live in Europe now.

*James Joyce's "Circe" manuscript*

But Eleanor is concerned about the precious parcel in her luggage.

Her adventurous daughter Sylvia, 34, has not only opened her own business, a bookstore on the Left Bank of Paris called Shakespeare and Company, but now she's become a publisher too. She's offered to publish the scandalous novel, *Ulysses,* by Irish ex-patriate writer James Joyce, 39. Earlier this year, a court in New York declared excerpts which appeared in a magazine to be obscene, so no decent publisher will touch it.

Sylvia snapped up the opportunity.

A wealthy New York lawyer, John Quinn, 51, is buying copies of the handwritten manuscript to keep some cash flowing to Joyce. Just last month he received in the mail the text of the "Circe" section of the novel.

Good thing. Back in Paris, one of the many typists working on the book had her copy seized by her outraged husband and thrown into the fire! Apparently he agreed with the New York court. The typist salvaged what she could, but Joyce and Beach implored Quinn to send his copy back so it can be typed.

That's where Eleanor comes in. For the past few weeks she has been calling Quinn asking if he would entrust her with the manuscript to bring along on her voyage over.

He has consistently said no. Over and over again. And, as she pointed out to her daughter, he used "language unfit" for a minister's wife like Mrs. Beach.

Finally, the rude man agreed to have the pages of the manuscript photographed so Mrs. Beach could take the pictures with her instead.

Eleanor is well aware of the importance of the parcel in her luggage which she is bringing to Paris.

# ❧ EARLY MAY, 1921 ❧
## LEFT BANK, PARIS

*Bryher*

Everyone's coming to Paris...

American ex-patriate writer **Robert McAlmon**, 26, and his new British wife, Bryher, 26, have moved to Paris after visiting her wealthy family in London for their honeymoon.

**Bob** is planning to use his wife's inheritance, along with the allowance her family is giving him, to start a small publishing company, Contact Press, named after the *Contact* magazine he founded in New York late last year with a fellow poet.

When they first got to Paris, the **McAlmons** made a point of visiting the English-language bookstore, Shakespeare and Company on the Left Bank, and signing up as members of the lending library. They are using the shop as an address and stopping by every day to pick up their mail.

There is a real buzz in the store. The owner, also an American ex-pat, Sylvia Beach, 33, is working on a major project. She has offered to publish *Ulysses,* the latest work by Irish novelist James Joyce, 39, even though excerpts from it were recently ruled obscene in New York when they appeared in *The Little Review* there.

**McAlmon** and Joyce have become good friends. In London, **Bob** received a letter of introduction from Harriet Shaw Weaver, 44, one of his benefactors and owner of The Egoist Press, to meet the Irish novelist. He and Bryher have been supporting the Joyces with a $150 per month stipend, and **McAlmon** is helping to type parts of the—extremely messy—manuscript as Joyce writes it.

At the shop, everyone is pitching in to mail out a prospectus and order forms to potential subscribers to *Ulysses,* which is planned to come out in the fall. Orders are coming in. Beach records them in separate green record books for each country. The biggest single order—25 copies—has come from the Washington Square Bookshop in Greenwich Village, one of the original defendants in the obscenity case. Bryher is helping out by setting up a system of alphabetical pigeonholes for the incoming mail.

At night, **McAlmon** and Joyce, sometimes joined by French writer Valery Larbaud, 39, make the rounds of the clubs and dance halls. They particularly like Gipsy's on the Boulevard St. Michel. **McAlmon** staggers from table to table getting drunken patrons to fill out order forms for the novel. He brings what he calls another "Hasty Bunch" of signed forms to the shop on his way home early in the morning, after having been thrown out of the last club along with his two comrades. Sylvia can barely make out the scrawly handwriting.

**McAlmon** is popular on the Left Bank for his charming personality, of course, but also because he can buy the drinks. Lots of drinks. He and Larbaud had to bring Joyce home one night in a wheelbarrow. Joyce's partner and mother of his children, Nora Barnacle, 37, admonished him,

> Jim, what is it all ye find to jabber about the nights you're brought home drunk for me to look after? You're dumb as an oyster now, so God help me."

# ❧ MAY 17, 1921 ☙
## HOTEL PENNSYLVANIA, 401 SEVENTH AVENUE, NEW YORK CITY, NEW YORK

This all started back in February. Ruth Hale, 34, journalist and theatrical agent, received her passport in the mail from the U. S. State Department. Made out to "Mrs. Broun."

*Ruth Hale*

Well, the only "Mrs. Broun" in her Upper West Side house is the cat. So she refused to accept it.

Four years ago, when she agreed to marry fellow journalist and sportswriter **Heywood Broun**, 32, they agreed she would keep her surname. Which hasn't been easy. She fights with authorities every time she has to sign anything.

One of her friends, *New York Times* reporter Jane Grant, 28, is waging the same battle, with some support from her husband, magazine editor **Harold Ross**, also 28.

The two couples lunch regularly in midtown at the Algonquin Hotel, with other writers and critics from the city's major newspapers. And they are often part of late night poker games at **Ross** and Grant's apartment. Which **Ross** expects Grant to clean up after.

At least Hale, who insists on living on a separate floor from **Broun** in their house, had him agree to split the child care raising their son, Heywood Hale Broun, three.

The talk at lunch always turns to Hale and Grant complaining about the injustice of being expected to give up their surnames. A few weeks ago, **Ross** was sick of listening to them and said,

**❝** Why don't you just go hire a hall?"

*Jane Grant*

So here they are at the Hotel Pennsylvania for the founding meeting of the Lucy Stone League.

They have managed to cajole some of their other lunch buddies to join, including **FPA [Franklin Pierce Adams]**, 39, the top columnist in Manhattan; Neysa McMein, 33, an illustrator whose apartment has become a favorite hang out for the group; and Beatrice Kaufman, 26, publicist and wife of the playwright **George S Kaufman**, 31. **Broun** joins; **Ross** doesn't. And one of their woman friends from the Algonquin gang also says no: **Dorothy Rothschild Parker**, 27, tells them,

**❝** I married *to* change my name."

The Lucy Stone League honors the 19th century suffragist who was the first American woman to use her birth name even after she married. Guess she never needed a passport.

With this group of writers and PR women involved, the League won't have trouble getting the word out. However, the *Times* reporter is referring to them as "The Maiden Namers."

Just nine months ago American women finally secured through the 19th Amendment the right to vote in all elections. Among the rights the League's founders—Hale as President,

*Ad for the Hotel Pennsylvania*

Grant as Secretary-Treasurer—feel they will have to fight for include opening a bank account, holding a copyright, registering at a hotel, and signing up for a store account, an insurance policy, or a library card.

# ❧ MAY 20, 1921 ❧

## GROSVENOR GALLERY, BOND STREET, LONDON

The opening of the "Nameless Exhibition" here, sponsored by *The Burlington Magazine,* has caused a bit of controversy.

The organizers, including *Burlington* founder and former editor **Roger Fry**, 54, and Professor of Fine Art at the Slade School Henry Tonks, 59, decided to make a brave move and hang a whole exhibit of paintings with no artists' names attached. Not on the walls; not in the catalogue. They want to strike a blow against the cult of personality which has gathered around some artists.

*Poster for Nameless Exhibition by Roger Fry*

Included are works by three of **Roger's** Bloomsbury friends, his former lover **Vanessa Bell**, about to turn 42, her partner **Duncan Grant**, 36, and Slade School grad, Dora Carrington, 28.

**Fry** can't wait to tell **Vanessa** that Tonks has hung one of her works, *Visit,* quite prominently, unaware that it is by a woman. Tonks goes on incessantly about how women painters are always imitating men.

Even though this is one of Carrington's first important exhibits, all she is thinking about is her wedding tomorrow.

❦

Carrington has spent the past four years living with and in love with Bloomsbury writer **Lytton Strachey**, 41, at Mill House in Tidmarsh, Berkshire. Carrington is well aware that **Lytton** is openly gay, but he is fond of her and is providing her the literary education she lacks. In exchange she paints and runs the household.

About three years ago, into this lovely arrangement walked big, strong, Ralph Partridge, 27, an Oxford friend of Carrington's younger brother. He's fallen in love with Carrington and moved into Tidmarsh. And **Lytton** is interested in him.

Now that Ralph has gainful employment—working as an assistant at the Hogarth Press operated by Bloomsbury regulars **Virginia Woolf**, 39, and her husband **Leonard**, 40—he can just afford to take a wife. Although **Lytton** is paying for the wedding.

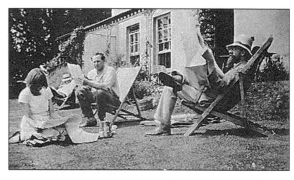

**Lytton** has spent the past two months convincing Carrington to take the plunge. And the **Woolfs** approve also.

Carrington finally agreed. She cries each night and writes **Lytton** long love letters. Ralph knows she's not in love with him. Carrington feels this is the way to keep the three together.

*Dora Carrington, Ralph Partridge and Lytton Strachey*

**Lytton** is already in Venice. The newlyweds are going to meet up with him there in a few weeks on their honeymoon.

# ✷ MAY 25, 1921 ✷
## 1 PM, GMT, CUSTOM HOUSE QUAY;
### AND DUNDRUM, DUBLIN

About 100 Irish Republican Army [IRA] Volunteers who have been milling around outside the Custom House, on the Liffey in Dublin City Centre, rush the building and herd the staff into the main hall. A truck loaded with supplies pulls up, and members of the IRA Dublin Brigade scatter oil and cotton all over the building and set it on fire.

Within about 10 minutes, British police arrive in three trucks and exchange fire with the IRA Volunteers inside the building. After about a half hour, the IRA's ammunition runs out. The rebels are shot by the British as they run away.

Staff inside who have been held hostage by the Volunteers walk out of the building, hands raised, waving white handkerchiefs.

Seven civilians are killed and 11 wounded. 100 people are arrested, mostly IRA members.

*The Custom House on fire*

The Fire Brigade arrives late because they have been held at their station by other IRA bands. Local government records from throughout the country, dating back to 1600, had been transferred to the Custom House for safekeeping. They are all destroyed.

Tonight, the building, one of the most beautiful in Ireland, called by the IRA the "seat of an alien tyranny," is still burning.

❦

Six miles south, in the Dublin suburb of Dundrum, Lolly Yeats, 53, co-owner of Cuala Press with her brother, poet **William Butler Yeats**, 55, is disgusted by this War of Independence raging all around.

Just yesterday she wrote to her father in New York City about the horrible IRA ambush 10 days ago outside of Galway, of British officers and their friends, which left three dead. The only survivor is Margaret Gregory, 37, widowed daughter-in-law of **Lady Augusta Gregory**, 69, co-founder with **Willie** of Dublin's Abbey Theatre.

Margaret and her British friends were leaving a tennis party when the IRA jumped out and began shooting at their car. Lolly can't understand why on earth Margaret has been keeping company with British military officers?! Might as well wear a target on her back.

**Lady Gregory** was in England at the time of the ambush but returned to the west of Ireland as soon as she heard. When the police questioned Margaret about the identity of the attackers, **Augusta** cautioned them that Margaret doesn't recognize any of the local country folk.

*Re-enactment of the Ballyturn ambush*

Lolly has heard about the IRA's burning of the Custom House today. What a waste. The IRA calls it a victory but what about the loss of all those killed and arrested?

She wrote to her father that what upsets her most is her women neighbors having their houses raided by the British, searching for their sons who have supposedly joined the IRA.

And the damned military curfew that the Brits have imposed has totally ended any social life. No more evenings in the theatre.

# ✂ MAY, 1921 ✂

## EN ROUTE TO AND IN PARIS

Everyone's coming to Paris…

*Sherwood and Tennessee Anderson*

Novelist **Sherwood Anderson**, 44, and his wife Tennessee, 47, are sailing to Europe for the first time. **Anderson's** third book, *Winesburg, Ohio,* was a big hit two years ago, and he's been working at an ad agency in Chicago, but the **Andersons** wouldn't have been able to afford this trip on their own. **Sherwood's** benefactor, journalist and music critic Paul Rosenfeld, just turned 31, is accompanying them and paying for **Sherwood's** expenses at least. He wants to introduce them around to the other American ex-patriate writers and artists in Paris this summer.

✂

Novelist **F. Scott Fitzgerald**, 24, and his wife Zelda, 20, are also sailing to Europe for the first time.

Their first stop will be London where, thanks to a letter of introduction from **Scott's** Scribner's editor, Maxwell Perkins, 36, they plan to meet with one of Scribner's other legendary authors, John Galsworthy, 53.

But the **Fitzgeralds** are mostly looking forward to the next leg of their journey—Paris. They plan to visit with one of their New York friends who has been living there since January as the foreign correspondent for *Vanity Fair,* poet Edna St. Vincent Millay, 29.

**Scott** had thought of writing a European diary, but Perkins discouraged him so he will work on a new novel instead. His first, *This Side of Paradise,* did well for Scribner's, and he recently handed Perkins the finished manuscript of the second, *The*

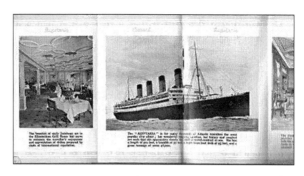

RMS Aquitania *brochure*

*Beautiful and Damned,* to get the money to pay for these tickets.

However, Zelda is about four months pregnant. She's been feeling sick a lot lately and this sea voyage on the *RMS Aquitania* isn't helping.

🙣◦🙥

English painters **Vanessa Bell**, about to turn 42, and her partner **Duncan Grant**, 36, are sailing over from London to Paris again. This is their usual spring and/or summer trip. This time they plan to visit with two of the painters whom they admire, Andre Derain, 40, and Pablo Picasso, 39, both of whom they met at a Gordon Square party two summers ago. **Duncan** is bringing along one of his current lovers.

🙣◦🙥

On the Left Bank, ex-pat English-language bookshop owner Sylvia Beach, 34, is looking forward to attending a play reading tonight a few blocks away at the French-language bookshop of her partner, Adrienne Monnier, 29.

Today, May 28th, the *Paris Tribune,* European edition of the *Chicago Tribune,* is running a big feature article about Sylvia and her store, Shakespeare and Company, written by a friend.

**" " Literary Adventurer.

American Girl Conducts Novel Bookstore Here"**

It includes pictures of Sylvia and refers to her as "an attractive as well as a successful pioneer."

Chicago Tribune *Paris edition nameplate*

What's most important is that the article mentions Sylvia's biggest project to date: Her publication of *Ulysses,* the notorious novel by ex-pat Irish writer James Joyce, 39. Excerpts printed in an American magazine have already been ruled to be obscene, and this kind of publicity just increases the drama around her upcoming publishing event.

The *Tribune* article warns that

**" " Its present publication may mean that Miss Beach will not be allowed to return to America."**

Who cares, thinks Sylvia. Everyone's coming to Paris.

# ❧ MAY, 1921 ❧
## HOWARD UNIVERSITY, WASHINGTON, D. C.

The May issue of the Howard University magazine, *The Stylus,* is out and Zora Neale Hurston, 30, is feeling so proud.

Zora never even thought she would get into Howard, let alone finish her associate degree last year. She was one of the first women chosen for the new sorority, Zeta Phi Beta, and her grades have been strong.

*Zora Neale Hurston at Howard University*

She not only has a poem published in this issue, but also her first short story, "John Redding Goes to Sea." That means she is now accepted into the university's prestigious literary club, also called The Stylus. Quite a coup. The professor who founded the group, Dr. Alain Locke, 35, chair of the philosophy department, is the only African-American ever chosen to be a Rhodes Scholar.

Her story is about African-Americans in the small, all-Black town where she grew up, Eatonville in Orange County, Florida. Zora feels that this is a community few authors write about. She's starting to think that she might pursue writing rather than anthropology as a career.

# ❧ EARLY JUNE, 1921 ❧
## 63RD STREET MUSIC HALL, NORTH OF BROADWAY, NEW YORK CITY, NEW YORK

S*huffle Along*, the first Broadway production in over a decade that has all African-Americans as producers, writers, and performers, is doing such bang up business in its first week that there are traffic jams each night before the curtain goes up.

*Noble Sissle and Eubie Blake*

With music and lyrics by Noble Sissle, 31, and Eubie Blake, 34, the revue is based on their vaudeville act, and they even wear their vaudeville tuxedos when they perform at the end of the second act.

As producers, Blake and Sissle had no trouble finding talent for *Shuffle Along*. The cast is terrific. In the auditions they found one 15-year-old who was fabulous but still too young for Broadway. They told Josephine Baker to come back next year when she turns 16.

The most amazing aspect, however, is that so many people—white and Black—are willing to find their way up here to see an all-Black musical. Blake and Sissle are glad that they finally secured a theatre, but it's not a great location. This music hall is surrounded by garages and auto parts stores and so small it doesn't even have a proper orchestra pit. Blake says,

❝ It isn't Broadway, but we made it Broadway."

*Shuffle Along* is a hit. Audiences are humming "I'm Just Wild About Harry," sung by the star—and Eubie's girlfriend—Lottie Gee, 34, as they walk out of the theatre. Sissle was nervous about how the opening night crowd would accept the tender love scene between the two Black leads, featuring the song "Love Will Find a Way." He and Blake watched from near the exit door, ready to flee. But the audience called for an encore!

*You can hear Eubie Blake and his Shuffle Along Orchestra, here.*
*https://www.youtube.com/watch?v=SmsTrhxQTGI.*

*and a piece from National Public Radio [NPR] about the centenary of the opening of Shuffle Along, here. https://www.npr.org/2021/05/23/998962830/shuffle-along-changed-musical-theater-100-years-ago*

# ❀ JUNE 6, 1921 ❀
## LINCOLN UNIVERSITY,
## CHESTER COUNTY, PENNSYLVANIA

U.S. President Warren G. Harding, 55, just three months in office, spent the past weekend at the White House concerned about what message he needs to send. He decided to accept this invitation to give the commencement address at Lincoln University this Monday.

Before sunrise, he and his wife Florence, 60, drove about 45 miles from Valley Forge, Pennsylvania, where they had stayed overnight with a friend, to this campus, outside of Oxford, Pennsylvania, the first all-Black degree-granting institution in the country.

The four cars carrying his entourage stop first at the granite arch on campus, where he helps to dedicate the memorial to Lincoln alumni who fought and died in the Great War.

The faculty and students of the "Black Princeton," as the school is known, are immensely proud to have a sitting president of the United States deliver their commencement address. They feel it is the high point of the university's 67-year history.

*President Harding at Lincoln University*

Speaking without notes, Harding addresses the students as "my fellow countrymen" and stresses the importance of education in solving racial problems. But he cautions that government alone cannot "take a race from bondage to citizenship in half a century."

*The damage to the Greenwood neighborhood of Tulsa, Oklahoma*

Then he turns his remarks to the most pressing issue in the country: The massacre of at least 39 citizens in the all-Black neighborhood—called "The Black Wall Street"—in Tulsa, Oklahoma, just five days ago. Offering a prayer for the city, Harding says,

❝ Despite the demagogues, the idea of our oneness as Americans has risen superior to every appeal to mere class and group. And so, I wish it might be in this matter of our national problem of races...God grant that, in the soberness, the fairness, and the justice of this country, we never see another spectacle like it."

When he is finished, the President congratulates and shakes the hand of each individual graduate.

# ❧ JUNE 10, 1921 ❧
## FONTANA VECCHIA, TAORMINA, SICILY, ITALY

Today is the day. English ex-patriate writer David Herbert Lawrence, 35, on his 20-minute walk from his hilltop house in to town, realizes that today is the day his novel *Women in Love* is being published in the United Kingdom. What a long and circuitous journey.

Lawrence had conceived of this novel during the Great War. But then had written and published six years ago what he thought of as part one, *The Rainbow,* in both the US and the UK.

Well, of course, the Brits had gone ballistic and banned it under the Obscene Publications Act of 1857.

1857.

Did they realize it is now the 20th century?!

Angry, Lawrence sat down and wrote *Women in Love* as a response, telling his literary agent,

*D. H. and Frieda Lawrence*

❝ You will hate it and no one will publish it. But there, these things are beyond us."

Actually, his American publisher, Thomas Seltzer, 46, was willing to take a chance and published it last November. But only in a US private edition costing $15 each. Bit of a narrow audience. Lawrence argued that he didn't want it to be released that way, but eventually gave in. The title page doesn't even include the publisher's name. Just "Private Printing for Subscribers Only."

Seltzer has told Lawrence that his books are selling quite well in the States, even in a bad year for publishing. However, after the uproar over *The Rainbow* in the UK, Seltzer doesn't want to take any chances bringing out *Women in Love* over there.

Martin Secker, 39, has shouldered the burden with his publishing company. Fear of the censors has led Secker to make a few discreet edits. But *Women in Love* is scheduled to be unleashed on the public today.

Lawrence and his wife, Frieda, 41, have been in self-imposed exile from England for the past four years. Because Frieda is German, their English neighbors had suspected them to be spies. Ridiculous. And also, he writes dirty books.

The couple have been traveling throughout Europe, mostly Germany—which seemed to Lawrence to be "so empty...as if uninhabited...life empty: no young men"—and Italy. Last year they settled in this Sicilian town. At the beginning of this month, visiting Frieda's family in Germany, he finished *Aaron's Rod,* his third novel in the series about his home country, the English midlands.

*Fontana Vecchia*

Seltzer feels that right now Lawrence has too many books out in the US market, so he is going to hold publication of *Aaron's Rod* until next year.

David and Frieda are getting antsy. In Italy, he has been writing very little. He is hopeful that excerpts from his travelogue *Sea and Sardinia* will appear in the American *Dial* magazine later this year.

Their passports will need to be renewed soon. Lawrence feels it may be time to move on to the next adventure.

# ❧ JUNE, 1921 ❧
## EN ROUTE TO AND IN PARIS

Everyone's coming to Paris…

Harvard undergraduate **Virgil Thomson**, 24, is thrilled to be headed to Paris for the first time on the European tour of the Harvard Glee Club—the first such extensive tour by any American university choral group. He's the accompanist, but also an understudy for the conductor, Dr. Archibald T. "Doc" Davison, 37, who has led the 63-year-old choir for the past two years.

*Harvard Glee Club logo*

The Glee Club will be traveling through France for four weeks, then three more weeks in Switzerland and Italy. Playing 23 concerts at major venues in 12 major cities.

But what **Virgil** is looking forward to most is staying on in Paris after the Glee Club goes back to America.

*Nadia Boulanger*

This tour came about because French history professor Bernard Fay, 28, who had been at Harvard, managed to get the French Foreign Office to issue an official invitation to the Club.

In addition to meeting their steamer when they dock at 2 am, Fay will be able to introduce **Virgil** to those in Paris whom he needs to know, particularly French composers such as Darius Milhaud, 28, and Francis Poulenc, 22.

Thanks to a teaching fellowship, **Virgil** will be staying on in Paris for a full year to study composition with renowned composer and teacher Nadia Boulanger, 33. What an opportunity. He'll be staying with a French family at first, but then hopes to find his own flat near Boulanger's studio on the Right Bank.

⁂

Artist Marcel Duchamp, 33, on the other hand, is heading for home.

Marcel has been living in and around New York City for the past six years. After his painting *Nude Descending a Staircase* was such a big hit at the 1913 Armory Show, he was able to finance a trip to the States and leverage his newfound fame to acquire artist friends and valuable patrons, Walter, 43, and Louise Arensberg, 42. As owners of the building where he has a studio, the Arensbergs agreed to take one of Duchamp's major paintings, *The Large Glass,* in lieu of rent.

Duchamp's English wasn't good at first, but supporting himself by giving French lessons helped to improve it quickly.

Marcel feels it's time to go back home to Paris. Even just for a few months.

⁂

After a stop in London, the **Fitzgeralds** are now in Paris.

In England, **Scott**, 24, wasn't particularly impressed with his fellow Scribner's novelist John Galsworthy, 53, whom he met at his home in Hampstead.

**Scott** and his wife Zelda aren't really impressed with Paris either. The managers of the Hotel Saint-James-et-d'Albany where they are staying complain when Zelda blocks the elevator door on their floor so it will be available for her.

The real problem with this trip, though, is that Zelda is sick all the time. And pregnant.

American novelist **Sherwood Anderson**, 44, and his wife, Tennessee, 47, on the other hand, are having a ball on their first trip to Europe. They've seen a terrific exhibit of works by Spanish artist Pablo Picasso, 39. Visited Chartres. Met American ex-patriate poet Ezra Pound, 35. They were more impressed by the Chartres cathedral than they were by Pound.

What **Sherwood** is really looking forward to, however, is using the letter of introduction he just received from the American owner of Shakespeare and Company, Sylvia Beach, 34, to meet her friend and fellow American, writer **Gertrude Stein**, 47. He has read some of **Stein's** pieces in the "little mags"

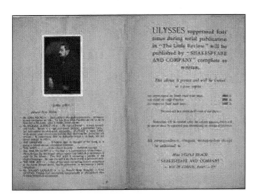

that he's found back in Chicago and has learned so much from her radical style.

In exchange, **Sherwood** is helping Sylvia send out prospectuses to all the Americans he can think of, soliciting subscriptions for her upcoming publication of *Ulysses,* the scandalous novel by the Irish ex-patriate, James Joyce, 39.

*Prospectus for* Ulysses

Recent Yale graduate Thornton Wilder, 24, and his sister, Isabel, 21, both writers, have been in Paris since the beginning of the month. During his recent eight-month residency at the American Academy in Rome, where he studied archaeology and Italian, Thornton started on his first novel, *The Cabala.*

Now that they are in Paris, Thornton and Isabel are signed up as members of Shakespeare and Company's lending library and they have made friends with Sylvia, thanks to a letter of introduction he carried from his friend, poet Stephen Vincent Benet, 22.

Sylvia has offered to introduce Wilder to Joyce, whom he has seen in her shop.

Thornton refused. Joyce always looks as though he doesn't want to be interrupted.

Right now, Thornton's biggest concern is finding a new place to live. The Hotel du Maroc, where they have been since they arrived, is crawling with bedbugs.

# ❧ EARLY SUMMER, 1921 ❧
## 27 RUE DE FLEURUS, PARIS

❝ He is so anxious to know you, for he says you have influenced him ever so much and that you stand as such a great master of words,"

reads the letter of introduction that Sylvia Beach, 34, owner of the Left Bank

bookshop Shakespeare and Company has sent to **Gertrude Stein**, 47, about their visiting fellow American, novelist **Sherwood Anderson**, 44. **Gertrude** and her partner, **Alice B. Toklas**, also 44, instantly decide that they would love to meet him.

A few days ago, Beach had found **Anderson** looking at his own book, *Winesburg, Ohio,* in the display window of her shop, and invited him in. Even after having great success two years ago with that collection of stories focused on the residents of one town, he still works in an ad agency back in Chicago. But a benefactor agreed to pay his expenses for this first trip to Europe. **Anderson** has

*27 rue de Fleurus*

read some of **Stein's** work in obscure American publications and has been impressed by her radical approach to writing.

**Anderson** and his wife Tennessee, 47, arrive at 27 rue de Fleurus, anticipating being in the presence of greatness. **Alice** is out running errands, but they talk at length with **Gertrude** about writing and writers. **Sherwood** tells her how much her writing has meant to him, and how it gave him confidence to keep going.

When **Alice** comes back, **Gertrude** tells her how impressed she is with **Anderson**. She has been writing for years but has few publications and little recognition. **Sherwood** praising her work means so much to her.

**Gertrude** and **Alice** hope that **Sherwood** will be **Stein's** link to the publishing world in America.

This summer, everyone's coming to Paris…

*NB: The first meeting of Stein, Toklas and Anderson is where I mark in my research the beginning of the Americans in Paris salon.*

# ❧ JUNE 22, 1921 ❧
## LEFT BANK, PARIS

American poet Edna St. Vincent Millay, 28, is having dinner with two of her friends visiting from New York, hit novelist **F. Scott Fitzgerald**, 24, and his wife, Zelda, 20, on their first trip to Europe.

They want to meet up with **Scott's** friend from his days at Princeton University, Edmund "Bunny" Wilson, 26, just arrived in Paris from New York.

*Edna St. Vincent Millay's passport*

"Poor Bunny," as she calls him, had eagerly found Millay as soon as he showed up two days ago. Edna made sure that, when Bunny came to her hotel room, on the rue de l'Universite, she was dressed in a demure black dress, at her typewriter, surrounded by neatly stacked manuscripts, evidence that she is indeed working. After all, Millay is living here as the foreign correspondent for *Vanity Fair,* thanks to Bunny, managing editor of the magazine.

Since she has been here, Edna has only written to Bunny once, sending him one of her poems. He must know that their relationship is over; he's been seeing someone else, an actress. But it's pretty clear he came to Paris mostly to meet up with Millay.

As they chatted, Edna started feeling more comfortable, so she confided in Bunny that she is planning to marry Englishman George Slocombe, 27, special correspondent for the *London Daily Herald*. Well, as soon as he divorces his wife and kids in the suburbs. She wants to move to England with

*Edmund Wilson*

him. Edna has explained to George that Bunny is "just a friend" from New York.

Meanwhile, Bunny has moved from his Right Bank [i.e., posh] hotel to a pension just a few blocks away from her hotel, on this side of the River Seine, the Left Bank [i.e., funky].

**Scott** and Zelda are staying on the Right Bank. They say they'll try to find Bunny. Edna is in no hurry.

The **Fitzgeralds** haven't been enjoying this trip. England. Italy. France—They've been disappointed all along. Zelda has been sick because she's pregnant. Now they are looking forward to going home, albeit via England again. They might move to Zelda's home state of Alabama next. They feel that they are done with Europe.

Edna feels as though she is just getting started.

# ✻ JUNE 25, 1921 ✻
## SHILLINGFORD, BERKSHIRE, ENGLAND;
## DUNDRUM, DUBLIN; AND
## MANHATTAN, NEW YORK CITY, NEW YORK

Irish poet and playwright **William Butler Yeats**, just turned 56, living in Shillingford, Berkshire, England, with his pregnant wife, is convinced that he has finally gotten his father to agree.

His Dad, painter John Butler "JB" Yeats, 82, has been living in New York City for 13 years. He went over on holiday and just decided to stay. Despite constant entreaties from his son and daughters.

**Yeats'** friend, Irish-American lawyer John Quinn, 51, has been looking out for JB, but he's running out of patience with the older man's demands. And, with a baby on the way, **Willie** can't afford to keep covering Dad's expenses.

**Willie** has issued an ultimatum and Quinn is booking JB passage back to Ireland for this fall.

**Yeats'** sister Lolly, 53, a publisher and teacher, is thrilled that Dad will be coming to live with her and her sister Lily, 54, an embroiderer, in the Dundrum suburb of south Dublin. They have painted his room and bought him a new bed and mattress.

Yesterday Lolly wrote to assure her father that in the intervening 13 years, his daughters have changed. They're no longer irritable and over-tired, and they look forward to just sitting and chatting with him. Their brother, **Willie**, however, is wondering whether Dad will be able to stick to a curfew.

However.

In Manhattan, JB Yeats is in no humor to go back to his family.

He has just read parts of **Willie's** family memoir, "Four Years," scheduled to appear in *The Dial* literary magazine. Dad has a big problem with at least one item in the text. Back when the family lived in the Bedford Park neighborhood of West London, young **Willie** left for two weeks to do some research in Oxford. In the memoir he describes the family as "enraged" at his absence.

*Yeats' family home in Bedford Park*

Not the way Dad recalls it. He remembers the loving family being supportive of this overgrown teenager.

Yesterday he wrote to **Willie**,

❝ As to Lily and Lollie, they were too busy to be 'enraged' about anything. Lily working all day…and Lolly dashing about giving lectures on picture painting and earning close on £300 a year…while both gave all their earnings to the house. And besides all this work, of course, they did the housekeeping and had to contrive things and see to things for their invalid mother…"

He admonishes his son for choosing a career writing plays and establishing Dublin's Abbey Theatre with **Lady Augusta Gregory**, 69, and other friends. If he were a good son he would have collaborated with his artist-father, and thereby helped both their careers.

And by the way, Dad isn't coming back.

*The W. B. Yeats Bedford Park Artwork Project, a community-led arts/education charity, is working to install a major contemporary sculpture, the first ever honouring Yeats in Britain, at the former Yeats family home. Find out more here. http://www.wbyeatsbedfordpark.com/*

# ⚜ LATE JUNE, 1921 ⚜
## 74 GLOUCESTER PLACE, MARYLEBONE, LONDON

Harriet Shaw Weaver, 44, owner of the Egoist Press, is somewhat relieved after reading the letter from Irish novelist James Joyce, 39, living in Paris, one of the writers she has been supporting for years.

A bit ago, two other writers she supports, Englishman Wyndham Lewis, 38, and American **Robert McAlmon**, 26, had both mentioned to her that their mutual friend Joyce uses some of the money she sends to him to fund a "lavish" lifestyle, meaning most evenings he ends up quite drunk. And she thought that she had been helping out his family.

Harriet is no prude. She is an active suffragist and has used her family inheritance [her maternal grandfather did quite well in the cotton trade] to support writers and artists, through the *Egoist* magazine and now her Egoist Press, as well as personally financing many creative individuals. She published excerpts from Joyce's *Ulysses* in her magazine even though they had to be printed abroad because English printers wouldn't touch the "obscene" text.

But she wrote to Joyce earlier this month to express her concerns about his drinking.

Harriet is pleased with his response.

Joyce writes that there are lots of rumors about the way he lives. He's a spy. He's addicted to cocaine. He's lazy. And mad. And even dying.

Joyce describes the technique he is using to write *Ulysses*:

❝ I have not read a work of literature for several years. My head is full of pebbles and rubbish and broken matches and bits of glass picked up 'most everywhere. The task I set myself technically in writing a book from 18 different points of view and in as many styles, all apparently unknown or undiscovered by my fellow

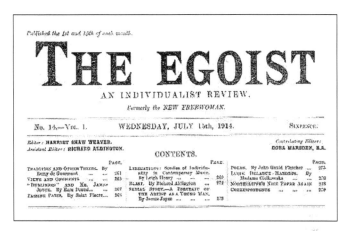

*Early issue of* The Egoist

tradesmen…would be enough to upset anyone's mental balance. I want to finish the book and try to settle my entangled material affairs. After that I want a good long rest in which to forget *Ulysses* completely. I now end this long rambling shambling speech having said nothing of the darker aspects of my detestable character."

However, at the end of the letter, Joyce confesses about his drinking,

66    Yet you are probably right."

Harriet is not sure. She and Joyce have been corresponding almost daily since she published his novel *A Portrait of the Artist as a Young Man* four years ago. Once she has begun to support an artist, she has never wavered.

But should she continue to invest her capital in an Irishman who drinks so much?

# ❧ JULY 2, 1921 ❧

## BOYLE'S THIRTY ACRES, JERSEY CITY, NEW JERSEY; AND TONY SOMA'S, WEST 49TH STREET, NEW YORK CITY, NEW YORK

Boxing promoter George "Tex" Rickard, 51, knew that bringing his client, world heavyweight champion Jack Dempsey, 26, into the ring to defend his title against world light heavyweight champion Georges Carpentier, 27, would draw a big crowd.

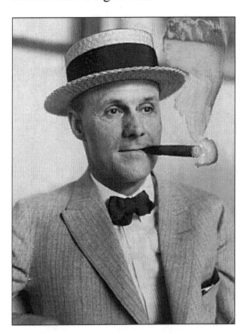

*Tex Rickard*

So big, in fact, that, rather than hold the bout in his usual venue, Madison Square Garden, Rickard has built this new facility, Boyle's Thirty Acres, across the river in Jersey City, New Jersey, to hold 90,000. Besides, he's been having a bit of trouble recently with the New York State Boxing Commission and Tammany Hall.

Dempsey has an almost 20-pound weight advantage over the Frenchman. But Rickard has spun the story for the newspapers so that this is seen as a fight between the handsome French war hero, Carpentier, and the American draft dodger [in reality, Dempsey received an exemption for family reasons] who recently divorced his wife. As a result, Tex has more women buying tickets for a boxing match than ever before.

The winner gets $300,000. The loser, $200,000.

Rickard is hoping that this will be the first million-dollar gate in boxing history. It is the first fight to be sanctioned by the newly organized National Boxing Association. And the first sporting event to be broadcast live in more than 60 cities across the country.

In a brownstone on West 49th Street, past an iron grille and a locked wooden door with a peephole, a group of revellers are drinking illegal booze out of big white coffee cups at tables covered with red checkered cloths.

Tony Soma's is the speakeasy of choice for the Manhattan writers and editors who lunch regularly a few blocks away at the Algonquin Hotel.

**Dorothy Parker**, 27, **Robert Benchley**, 31, and Robert Sherwood, 25, met when they worked together on *Vanity Fair* magazine. But since a bit of a tiff with management at the

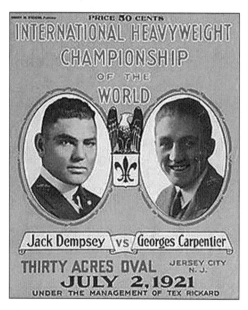

*Program from Dempsey Carpentier fight*

beginning of last year, **Dottie** has been free-lancing, and **Benchley** and Sherwood are editing the humor magazine *Life*.

On this Saturday of a long Fourth of July weekend, they are joined by friends just returned from their first holiday in Europe, novelist **F. Scott Fitzgerald**, 24, and his pregnant wife, Zelda, 20.

*Dempsey knocks out Carpentier*

In the *New York Evening World,* **Parker** and **Benchley's** friend, magazine illustrator Neysa McMein, 33, has sketched Carpentier, calling him "The Pride of Paris," commenting that Michelangelo "would have fainted for joy with the beauty of his profile."

Tonight they are all here to listen to the radio broadcast of the "Fight of the Century."

As they always do, **Benchley's** friends are urging the teetotaler to at least try some alcohol. How can he be so against something that he's never even tried? **Benchley** has taken the pledge to not drink and even voted *for* Prohibition.

But tonight, he figures, What the hey. He orders an Orange Blossom.

**Benchley** takes a few sips. He turns to **Parker** and says,

❝ This place should be closed down by the police."

Then he orders another.

By the end of the evening, Dempsey has defeated Carpentier in the fourth round.

*Orange Blossom cocktail*

And Orange Blossoms have defeated **Robert Benchley**.

# Recipe for an Orange Blossom

1 oz. gin
1 oz. fresh orange juice
1 tsp. powdered sugar
Orange peel

Shake gin, orange juice, and sugar over ice. Strain into
a cocktail glass. Garnish with flamed orange peel.

*This recipe from the Robert Benchley Society appears in*
Under the Table: A Dorothy Parker Cocktail Guide
*by Kevin C. Fitzpatrick [Guilford, CT: Lyons Press, 2013]*

# ❧ EARLY JULY, 1921 ❧
## 71 RUE DE CARDINAL LEMOINE, PARIS

Irish novelist James Joyce, 39, has been working hard to finish his controversial novel *Ulysses*. But now he is in incredible pain.

A few nights ago he was, as usual, out drinking with one of his supporters [financially and morally], American writer and owner of the Contact press, **Robert McAlmon**, 25. The two ex-pats were making the rounds of their favorite drinking places when Joyce suddenly fainted and went limp.

*71 rue de Cardinal Lemoine*

**McAlmon** brought him back home here, where he's been living for the past month, down the long gravelly driveway through the big iron gate, which requires a huge metal key.

The next morning, Joyce woke up with a severe attack of iritis. The pressure inside his eye had him rolling on the floor in pain.

Even having a light on is painful. Joyce is now forced to rest and recuperate in this terrific third-floor apartment belonging to one of his French fans, the poet Valery Larbaud, also 39. Larbaud is on holiday until October, so has offered this luxurious flat rent-free to the Joyce family. Of the 22 different addresses the Joyces have had while James has been working on *Ulysses,* this is definitely the most posh.

Joyce has been making good progress, but he's not sure that he will make the announced October publication date for his novel. This most recent eye attack will set him back. And there is another hold up from the printer. They are running out of certain letters that appear more in English than they do in French—e, h, w and y. Who knew?

# ✂ JULY, 1921 ✂
## EN ROUTE TO AND IN PARIS

Everyone's coming to Paris...

On board ship, steaming from the United States to France, Irish-American attorney John Quinn, 51, is finally starting to relax.

Leaving his successful law office behind to go on this holiday feels as though he has been let out of prison.

On previous European trips Quinn has focused on visiting with his friends in Dublin and London. This time he is going to spend the whole time in Paris. Specifically meeting with the artists and writers whom he has been supporting financially for the past few years.

Back in May he arranged through the secretary of state to get a passport for his representative [and lover] Mrs. Jeanne Foster, 42, to precede him and arrange meetings with art dealers and artists.

In particular he is looking forward to in-person dinners with...

*Constantin Brancusi, 45.* Quinn became familiar with the Romanian sculptor's work when he exhibited in the 1913 Armory Show, which Quinn helped to organize. Quinn has bought two versions of Brancusi's *Mlle. Pogany,* and keeps some of his works in the foyer of his Central Park West apartment. As Quinn wrote to the grateful artist earlier this year,

❝ I can't have too much of a beautiful thing."

*Gwen John, 45.* Quinn is her number one buyer. He bought one of the many versions of a portrait the Welsh painter did of *Mere Marie Poussepin,* the founder of the order of nuns Ms. John lives next door to in a Paris suburb. Quinn much prefers her work to that of her brother, painter Augustus John, 43, whom he stopped supporting a few years ago after a dispute.

*James Joyce, 39*. Quinn has been buying up the manuscript of Joyce's novel *Ulysses* as the ex-pat Irishman works on it. And he defended [pro bono, of course] the American magazine, *The Little Review,* which dared to publish "obscene" excerpts of the novel. Quinn is quite proud that he got the publishers off with a $100 fine and no jail sentence.

Now it's time to put legal issues behind him and enjoy Paris.

✂✁✄

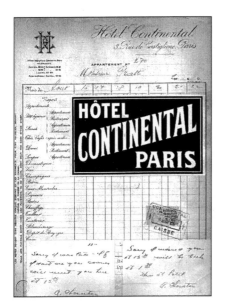

Scofield Thayer, 31, is in Paris en route to Vienna. He feels he can continue his position as editor and co-owner of the New York-based *The Dial* literary magazine while he is living in Europe. The international postal service and Western Union should make it easy enough for him to work remotely.

The foreign editor of *The Dial,* American ex-patriate poet Ezra Pound, 35, is hosting Thayer for his few days in Paris. Pound came to visit him at his hotel, the Hotel Continental on rue de Castiglione, and brought along another American poet, E. E. Cummings, 26, whom Scofield knew at Harvard. Cummings recently returned to Paris and is working on a novel about his experiences as an ambulance driver here during the Great War.

*Hotel Continental bill*

Most interesting, however, is the visit Pound arranged for Thayer to meet another American writer, **Gertrude Stein**, 47, and her partner **Alice B. Toklas**, 44, at 27 rue de Fleurus. They had just met one of *The Dial's* main contributors, **Sherwood Anderson**, 44, author of the successful collection of stories, *Winesburg, Ohio*. **Stein** and **Toklas** discussed with Thayer how impressed they are with **Anderson**, who is a big fan of **Gertrude's** work.

Now Scofield is ready to move on to the next leg of his trip: To Vienna and psychoanalysis treatment with Sigmund Freud, 65.

⚜

*Vanity Fair* managing editor Edmund Wilson, 26, after staying a few days in a hotel, has moved to this pension at 16 rue de Four.

Since arriving in Paris last month, Wilson has seen the object of his affections, American poet Edna St. Vincent Millay, 29, a few times. But it is clear to him that she is no longer interested. Edna has told him about her new lover, "a big red-haired British journalist," as

*16 rue du Four*

Wilson writes to his friend back at *Vanity Fair,* John Peale Bishop, also 29. He tells Bishop that Edna

❝ looks well…and has a new distinction of dress, but she can no longer intoxicate me with her beauty, or throw bombs into my soul."

Time to move on.

⚜

Over at the bookstore Shakespeare and Company, American owner Sylvia Beach, 34, has said goodbye to her new friend, novelist **Anderson**, whom she introduced to **Stein** and **Toklas** earlier this summer. He and his wife are headed to London and then back home to Chicago.

Sylvia also feels it's time to leave Paris, but just for a bit. She and her partner Adrienne Monnier, 29, are planning a short holiday. But first Sylvia wants to settle her bookshop in its new location.

# ❧ JULY 14, 1921 ❧
## NORFOLK COUNTY COURTHOUSE,
## DEDHAM, MASSACHUSETTS

The jury takes only three hours and a dinner break to convict the defendants, Nicola Sacco, 30, and Bartolomeo Vanzetti, 33, of first-degree murder in the robbery and shooting of two men at the Slater & Morrill Shoe Co. in Braintree, Massachusetts, last year.

Or were they really convicted for being Italian immigrant draft-dodging anarchists?

*Bartolomeo Vanzetti and Nicola Sacco*

Throughout the more than seven-week trial, Judge Webster Thayer, 64, fought with Sacco's California attorney, Fred H. Moore, 51. During one lunch recess, reporters heard the judge say,

❝ No long-haired anarchist from California can run this court!...You wait till I give my charge to the jury. I'll show them."

The men's alibis—on the day of the robbery and murders Sacco was having his passport renewed at the Italian consulate and Vanzetti was selling fish—are backed up by credible witnesses.

Of all the evidence, Judge Thayer kept coming back to a cap that was found at the scene and was supposed to be Sacco's. But, when Sacco tried it on in court, the cap didn't fit.

The prosecution did catch a few lies in the men's testimony, but neither Sacco nor Vanzetti ever denied being an anarchist.

Judge Thayer pronounces his sentence. Death by electric chair.

# ❧ LATE JULY, 1921 ❧
## EN ROUTE TO PARIS

Everyone's coming to Paris…

O n board ship, steaming from the United States to France, New York artist **Man Ray**, 30, is looking forward to his new life in Paris.

In a couple of days, once he docks and takes a train to the Gare St. Lazare, his French friend, fellow artist Marcel Duchamp, about to turn 34, will be there to meet him.

**Ray's** relocation is being funded by a Swiss-American collector he met through the Daniel Gallery in Manhattan. Ferdinand Howald, 65, is also supplying a $50 monthly allowance through the end of the year.

**Ray** [actually, Emmanuel Radnitzky] and Duchamp have been friends and chess rivals since Duchamp arrived in New York about six years ago. They worked on projects separately and together, including one issue of a magazine, *New York Dada.* **Ray** has been making a living photographing the acquisitions of collectors such as Howald and Irish-American lawyer John Quinn, 51. Duchamp decided to move back home to France some months ago.

Last year, **Ray**, Duchamp and American artist and heiress, Katherine Dreier, 43, founded *Societe Anonyme,* the "Museum of Modern Art," to present exhibits, symposiums and lectures. Dreier has been doing all the organizing and promoting.

*Katherine Dreier*

Recently. **Ray** gave a lecture for the *Societe* about Dada. As soon as he finished, Dreier got up, stood next to him, and told the audience she would now speak about modern art seriously.

Really.

When Howald offered him the opportunity to relocate and establish his career in Paris, he jumped at it. Time to leave New York behind...

# ❧ JULY 23, 1921 ❧
## *PICTURES* MAGAZINE, UNITED KINGDOM

Hollywood star Roscoe "Fatty" Arbuckle is on the cover of UK movie magazine, *Pictures*. He has had two hit films already this year, *Brewster's Millions* and *The Dollar-a-Year Man*.

Pictures *magazine*

# ❧ JULY 27, 1921 ❧
## RUE DE L'ODEON, PARIS

Everything is fitting in just right. American ex-patriate Sylvia Beach, 34, has relocated her shop, Shakespeare and Company, to this new location, a few blocks from where she originally opened almost two years ago.

One of her recent American visitors, the Irish-American lawyer and art collector, John Quinn, 51, had pronounced the previous shop "a hovel." Quinn is in the process of buying up the manuscript of *Ulysses,* the radical novel by Irish writer James Joyce, 39, which Sylvia is publishing this fall.

Quinn can be brusque. And rude.

But Beach and Joyce are glad he's chipping in with financial [and legal] support while Joyce finishes his monumental work.

*Sylvia Beach at her bookstore, 12 rue de l'Odeon*

Shortly after Quinn's visit, Sylvia's partner, Adrienne Monnier, 29, heard that the antiques dealer here in no. 12 wanted someone to take over her lease. Sylvia jumped at the chance.

A shoemaker, a corset maker, and a book appraiser to her left. An orthopaedic specialist, a music shop, and a nose spray manufacturer to her right. And Adrienne's own French-language bookshop, La Maison des Amis des Livres, right across the street at no. 7. A good fit.

Best of all, Adrienne's apartment is up the block at no. 18. Sylvia has already moved all her personal stuff in with Adrienne.

In addition to this great location just north of the Luxembourg Gardens, the new space is bigger and easier to find. Two rooms above the shop are included in the rent.

Quinn approves of the new place, happy that Joyce's *Ulysses* isn't "going to come out in that shanty."

Now that's she's all settled in, Sylvia and Adrienne are going away on a brief vacation.

*Adrienne Monnier at her bookstore, 7 rue de l'Odeon*

# ❧ END OF JULY, 1921 ❧
## 12 RUE DE BOULAINVILLIERS, PARIS

From the day he arrived in Paris, just a week or so ago, American ex-patriate artist **Man Ray**, 30, has been introduced to the most interesting creative people in the city.

His friend from their days in New York, French artist Marcel Duchamp, just turned 34, met him as promised at the Gare St. Lazare upon his arrival. The

*Surrealists at an exhibit opening, with Philippe Soupault and Andre Breton on the ladder*

next day they went to the Dada Café to meet the French legendary lights of that movement: Writer Andre Breton, 25; poet Paul Eluard, also 25; and writer Philippe Soupault, 23, who offered **Ray** an exhibit at his bookstore this coming fall. **Ray** has been turning down offers of shows from dealers in Germany and Belgium because it is important to him that his first European show is in Paris.

Duchamp also arranged for a place for **Ray** to live. The Romanian-French Dada poet Tristan Tzara, 25, is off traveling for three months so **Ray** has taken over his studio here in Passy. Based on the sign in the window **Ray** kept referring to this as the "Hotel Meuble," until Duchamp explains that *meuble* means that the rooms are furnished.

Into this cramped space, **Ray** has managed to squeeze a bed and three large cameras. He develops his photos in the tiny closet.

*Kiki of Montparnasse*

**Ray** has already secured a commission to photograph the autumn line of French couturier Paul Poiret, 42, but is actually more interested in sticking to portraiture.

At a party hosted by a wealthy visiting American couple, **Ray** struck up a conversation with an American writer he has heard a lot about—**Gertrude Stein**, 47. She has been living in Paris for almost 20 years now, and hosts salons with other ex-pats in her apartment at 27 rue de Fleurus which she shares with her partner, fellow San Franciscan **Alice B. Toklas**, 44.

**Ray** told **Stein** that he would like to photograph her and invited the two women to be the first to visit his little studio.

They are due any minute. As soon as their visit is over, **Ray** is going to meet up with a fascinating Frenchwoman he met recently, Alice Prin, 19, known around town as "Kiki, the Queen of Montparnasse."

# ✂ AUGUST 3, 1921 ✂
## CHICAGO, ILLINOIS; AND NEW YORK CITY, NEW YORK

Yesterday, everybody partied. The eight Chicago White Sox players accused of throwing the 1919 World Series and the 12-member jury all went out to an Italian restaurant to celebrate the players' acquittal.

Today, Judge Kenesaw Mountain Landis, 54, national commissioner of baseball, at the Commission's Manhattan offices, issued a statement banning all eight players from having any association with organized baseball. For life.

No playing in the minor leagues. No nominations to the Hall of Fame, no matter how deserved. No touring around the country with barnstorming teams, the way some of the eight have been doing since Landis suspended them last year.

Fans young and old have been sweating in the observers' seats in the hot courtroom for the past month. Even the trial judge seemed relieved when, after only three hours, the jury returned the not guilty verdict.

The Sox's star outfielder, "Shoeless" Joe Jackson, who turned 33 two

*The eight defendants in the "Black Sox" trial*

days before the trial began, and batted .375 in the series with one HR and six RBIs, said,

❝ When I walked out of Judge Dever's courtroom in Chicago…I had been acquitted by a 12-man jury in a civil courtroom of all charges, and I was an innocent man in the records."

Well, not exactly, Joe. The judge's name was Hugo Friend, and you and the others were found not guilty [not the same as innocent] in a *criminal* courtroom.

Whatever.

Judge Landis is not relieved. He believes that all eight men broke the rules of baseball. And he was named the first national commissioner—of both the National and American Leagues—last year to uphold the integrity of the game. Today he issues a statement which says in part:

❝ Regardless of the verdict of juries, no player who throws a ball game, no player who undertakes or promises to throw a ball game, no player who sits in confidence with a bunch of crooked ballplayers and gamblers, where the ways and means of throwing a game are discussed and does not promptly tell his club about it, will ever play professional baseball again."

No one is partying now.

# ❧ AUGUST 7 AND 8, 1921 ❧
## CHARLESTON FARMHOUSE; AND
## MONK'S HOUSE, RODMELL, ENGLAND

Art critic **Clive Bell**, 39, is at Charleston Farmhouse which he shares with his estranged wife, painter **Vanessa Bell**, 42, their two sons, Julian, 13, Quentin, about to turn 11, and assorted other family members and lovers.

**Clive** is writing to his current mistress, Mary Hutchinson, 32, back in London:

*Charleston Farmhouse*

❝ Nothing could exceed the monotony of life at Charleston except the pleasantness of that monotony…One comes down to breakfast as much before 10 as possible, hopes for letters, kills a wasp, smokes a pipe, contemplates nature, writes til lunch, reads the *Times,* goes for a walk, drinks tea, reads Proust, shaves, writes [a letter]…dines, lights a fire, smokes a cheroot, reads the Grenville memoirs, smokes a pipe, reads Proust, goes to bed. Sometimes it rains."

❧❧❧

About 10 miles away, at Monk's House in Rodmell, **Vanessa's** sister, novelist **Virginia Woolf**, 39, is quite unwell and has been losing weight. The sales of her latest book, *Monday or Tuesday,* have picked up, and she has started sleeping a bit better, without medication. But her current doctors have her on horrible "milk cures," which she can't abide.

**Virginia** has been unable to do any writing or see any guests for about two months, and confides to her diary,

66    What a gap! Two whole months rubbed out—These, this morning, the first words I have written—to call writing—for 60 days."

# ❧ AUGUST 10, 1921 ❧
## ABBEY THEATRE,
## 26/27 ABBEY STREET LOWER, DUBLIN

W ay back at the beginning of the century, when the Abbey Theatre was in its planning stages, the co-founder, poet and playwright **William Butler Yeats**, then 39, commissioned his friend and fellow Dubliner George Bernard Shaw, almost 10 years older than **Willie**, to write a play for the opening.

Shaw gave the Abbey *John Bull's Other Island,* a long political comedy about an Irishman and his English business partner who come to Ireland to look into developing some land. **Yeats** rejected it. The official reason was that he felt they wouldn't be able to find any actors to do the British characters justice. The real reason was that **Yeats** couldn't stand Shaw's argumentative style of playwriting.

George Bernard Shaw *by Alvin Langdon Coburn*

An edited version of the play premiered in London at the Royal Court Theatre that same year, 1904, and made Shaw a big hit with the Brits. Reports are that the king laughed so hard during a performance that he fell off his chair.

*John Bull's Other Island* was performed at another theatre in Dublin a few years later. And in 1909, when Abbey co-founder **John Millington Synge** died at age 37, both **Yeats** and his other Abbey cofounder, **Lady Augusta Gregory**, then 52, asked Shaw to step into the vacancy and help guide their theatre. He declined.

Now **Lady Gregory** is here to guide, what is basically her Abbey, 17 years after its opening. Tomorrow night they are putting on their seventh run of Shaw's political play.

Performances will be this Thursday and Saturday nights, and a Saturday matinee. In the cast is one of their new stars, Barry Fitzgerald, 33, in the role of Tim Haffigan, which he has done six times already.

*Royal Court Theatre, London*

Barry came to the Abbey a few years ago through his younger brother, who is both actor and stage manager for this production. Despite his breakthrough success last year in one of **Lady Gregory's** own plays, Barry still works his full-time civil service job. Where he is known by his given name, William Shields. Just to be safe.

*Abbey Theatre, Dublin*

In addition to his day job, Fitzgerald is appearing tonight and Friday in a new play by **Lady Gregory**, *Aristotle's Bellows,* and *Bedmates* by George Shiels, 40, his first play produced here.

**Augusta** feels that the theatre has reached a stable point in its history. But she is always on the lookout for new blood, both actors and playwrights.

# ❧ AUGUST 13, 1921 ❧
## FRAZEE THEATRE, 254 WEST 42ND STREET, NEW YORK CITY, NEW YORK

Opening night! **Marc Connelly**, 30, and **George S Kaufman**, 31, are here for the opening of their first major production, the three-act comedy *Dulcy*.

When they came to New York City—separately—from different western Pennsylvania cities to start their careers, this is exactly what each of them had in mind.

After getting a few things published in the city's daily newspapers, and working on a few theatre projects, last year **Connelly** and **Kaufman** were approached by two of the biggest Broadway producers, George C. Tyler, 53, and Harry Frazee, 41. The latter, owner of the Boston Red Sox, had within a few months last year sold his top player, legendary slugger Babe Ruth, 26, to the New York Yankees, and then bought this theatre.

DULCY (WHILE THE MUSIC PLAYS): "SHERRY'S! DELICIOUS! MOLASSES!"—*(Act 2)*

*Dulcy*

Tyler and Frazee wanted the playwrights to come up with a starring vehicle for a new British actress, Lynn Fontanne, 33, who has appeared in a couple of Broadway shows in the past few years.

The young pair turned to one of their friends in the group of writers they lunch with regularly at the nearby Algonquin Hotel, the most-read columnist in the city, **FPA [Franklin Pierce Adams]**, 39. In his *New York Tribune* column "The Conning Tower," **FPA** has created a recurring ditzy character called Dulcy, short for Dulcinea, after the heroine of *Don Quixote*. **Connelly** and **Kaufman** thought they could build something around her and offered **FPA** a 10% cut of the profits.

The show has been through try-outs in the Midwest—Indiana, Illinois—with **Kaufman** becoming ever more nervous as this night approached.

Two of their friends from the Algonquin lunches have said that they will review the play. They think **Heywood Broun**, 32, in the *Tribune* will probably like the tricky patter. But **Alexander Woollcott**, drama critic for the *Times* and **Kaufman's** boss there, has already said their play is probably not good enough for Fontanne.

Curtain going up…

# ❧ EARLY AUGUST, 1921 ❧
## EN ROUTE TO LONDON; AND BACK IN PARIS

Irish-American lawyer John Quinn, 51, is sailing back to New York, via London.

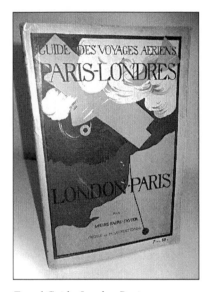

*Travel Guide, London-Paris*

On this European trip he has concentrated on just Paris—not Ireland, not England, which he visited in the past few years. And his focus has paid off.

He sent his ambassador [and lover], Mrs. Jeanne Foster, 42, ahead to arrange meetings with painters and their dealers.

She did a magnificent job. As a result, he's coming back with contracts to buy a sculpture and three paintings by Spaniard Pablo Picasso, 39, as well as works by Romanian painter and sculptor, Constantin Brancusi, 45, and French painters Andre Derain, 41, and Andre de Segonzac, 37.

More important to Quinn, he has developed personal friendships with the artists and their dealers.

Quinn also visited the English-language bookstore, Shakespeare and Company, owned by American ex-patriate Sylvia Beach, 34. He had advised her to move from her "shabby" location and Quinn approves of her new site on rue de l'Odeon. From here she plans to publish the monumental novel *Ulysses* by Irish ex-pat James Joyce, 39. Quinn is supporting Joyce financially by buying up the manuscript as it is written. Support the artist as well as the art.

Now Quinn is going back to the law office he thinks of as a prison.

✂✦✂

American novelist **Sherwood Anderson**, 44, and his wife Tennessee, 47, are heading back to his New York job, half-heartedly doing public relations for an independent movie company, via London.

His first trip to Europe has been what he'd dreamt of. After he visited Shakespeare and Company, Beach introduced him to Joyce and they had a few lunches together. Unfortunately, to get the conversation started the first time, **Anderson** asked Joyce what he thought of Ireland. Bad move.

**Anderson** has told Beach he will spread the word among his American literary friends about her upcoming publication of *Ulysses*. **Sherwood** gave Sylvia a list of names and as many addresses as he could remember for her to use to solicit subscriptions. He even added personal notes to the prospectuses she is sending out.

**Sherwood** thinks of the job waiting for him in New York as a joke. He still has some advertising accounts to bring in income, but he's not in a rush to go back to Chicago.

✂✦✂

American writer Edmund Wilson, 26, is heading back to his New York job, managing editor of *Vanity Fair,* via London. He enjoyed his time in Paris these past few weeks but doesn't think he really got a feel for the city.

Wilson spent most of his time tracking down and trying to lure back his former lover from New York City, poet Edna St. Vincent Millay, 29, living in Paris as *Vanity Fair's* European editor. Wilson has pushed and published her work in the magazine. But it's clear that Millay has moved on from Edmund. To some British newspaperman.

Last month Wilson wrote to one of the magazine's other editors,

 I found [Millay] in a very first-rate hotel on the Left Bank and better dressed, I suppose, than she has ever been before in her life. You were right in guessing that she was well cared for as she had never been before…[She] told me she wanted to settle down to a new life: She was tired of breaking hearts and spreading havoc."

⚜

*Sinclair Lewis*

American novelist Sinclair Lewis, 36, is heading *to* Paris *from* London.

Last year, his sixth novel, *Main Street,* was a bestseller. However, he lost out on the Pulitzer Prize to *The Age of Innocence* by Edith Wharton, 59. Apparently, *Main Street,* with its focus on the hypocrisy in a small Midwest town, didn't fit the jury's criteria of a novel "which shall best present the wholesome atmosphere of American life."

Lewis is bringing along another American writer whom he has just met in London, Harold Stearns, 30, whose book *America and the Young Intellectual* is coming out this year. Lewis plans to spend only a few days in Paris, but Stearns is going to stay on in Montparnasse, on the Left Bank.

⚜

Over on the Right Bank, American composer **Virgil Thomson**, 24, is settling into Paris and his temporary residence at the home of a French family on the rue de Provence.

At the beginning of the month, **Virgil** had bid a not-too-sad farewell to his fellow students in the Harvard Glee Club. The group has just completed a triumphant tour of France, with **Virgil** as accompanist. He was also the understudy for the conductor, and actually got a chance to step into the maestro's shoes one night. Now they are all heading back to America.

Except **Virgil**. With his well-earned scholarship, he is going to stay here in Paris for a whole year.

**Virgil** has already been to Shakespeare and Company in rue de l'Odeon and signed up for Beach's lending library. He is planning to move closer to the studio of Nadia Boulanger, 34, with whom he will be studying composition. His new residence at 20 rue de Berneis, a 10-minute walk from Boulanger, is in a less than desirable neighborhood. The street, and the building, are overwhelmed with what **Virgil** refers to as "daughters of joy."

# ❧ MID-AUGUST, 1921 ☙
## VIRGINIA HOTEL, 78 RUSH STREET,
## CHICAGO, ILLINOIS

Hadley Richardson, 29, visiting from St. Louis, feels that last night, at this posh hotel, for the first time, she "really got to know" her fiancé, free-lance journalist **Ernest Hemingway**, 22.

Hadley and **Ernest** had only seen each other twice before they got engaged this spring. But they write lots of letters to each other. And her **Ernesto** writes great letters.

When she came to Chicago earlier this year to meet his parents, Hadley had to bring a chaperone. Now that they are engaged, she has booked herself into the Virginia Hotel.

Hadley's sister, and quite a few of **Ernest's** friends, don't think this marriage is a good idea. But Hadley does. She has her own inheritance so doesn't have to depend on her family's good wishes.

Earlier this summer, she was trying to get **Hemingway** to tell her exactly how old he is and what exactly he did during the Great War. Hadley was putting together an announcement for their engagement party and told him to come up with

❝ a magnificent lie about your age in case anyone is curious enough to inquire—also tell me what events I can brag of without being a perfect fool about you."

**Ernie** says that he served in the Italian Army, and she is guessing that he turned at least 23 in July, when she gave him a typewriter for his birthday.

**Ernest's** day job involves editing a house organ, but he is trying to sell enough of his free-lance work to support himself without that income. Earlier this year he had a piece published about the Dempsey-Carpentier fight, building on his knowledge of boxing, but his poetry is continually rejected. He has stopped sending poems to *Poetry* magazine, hoping he will fare better with *The Dial*. They often publish poems by his friend and mentor, successful novelist **Sherwood Anderson**, 44. But so far—no luck.

Despite **Ernest's** evasiveness, and although he didn't come to visit her in St. Louis as he promised last New Year's Eve, Hadley is confident in his talent and is convinced that they are right for each other.

They were introduced at a party last fall by **Ernest's** friend, advertising copywriter Y. Kenley Smith, 33, and Hadley's friend, Smith's sister Kate, 29. But **Ernie** hasn't been getting on so well with Kenley these days. He and Hadley have decided that they are not going to move in with Smith and his wife after their wedding in a few weeks. And Kenley has been disinvited from the reception to be held at the Hemingway home in nearby Oak Park.

*Virginia Hotel, Chicago, Illinois*

# ❧ LATE AUGUST, 1921 ❧
## THE OLD PALACE, DEWAS, INDIA

Novelist Edward Morgan Forster, 42, wakes from a bad dream and feels relieved.

To attend this two-day festival celebrating the birth of Lord Krishna, Forster has moved from his three-room furnished suite to these rooms in the Old Palace, which offer a better view.

*Baby Krishna with his mother*

In his dream, Forster was back home in England with his mother Lily, 66, and his cat, Verouka. He dreamt that he had shown Verouka a mechanical doll that scared him. The cat was running round and round in the room above, making a terrible racket.

Forster's relief comes as he realizes the racket is from a steam engine that is generating electricity for the festival outside his window.

Morgan left England—and his annoying mother—on his second trip to India more than five months ago.

At the beginning of the year, Morgan wrote to his primary publisher that he would notify him if he ever got around to writing another book. His third and fourth novels, *A Room with a View* and *Howards End* have done well. But they were both published more than a decade ago.

Despairing of his mundane life and his inability to write, Forster prophesied to a friend,

❝ I shall go [on] some long and fantastic journey; but we do not yet know whither or when. I am so sad at the bottom of my mind."

Days later he received a cable from an old, dear friend, Sir Tukoji Rao IV, the Maharajah of Dewas State, 33, with whom he shares a January 1st birthday.

HH, as he is always referred to, decided—for some unfathomable reason— that Forster would be the ideal person to stand in for his private secretary who is going on six-month leave. HH offered Morgan paid return fare and expenses, 300 rupees per month, and his own young male concubine. Morgan had no idea what a "private secretary" would do. Still doesn't.

But Forster jumped at the chance for a "fantastic journey," renewed his passport and booked passage to India as soon as he could. Also, he knew his sea voyage would include a brief stopover in Port Said, Egypt, where he hoped to meet up with his Egyptian former lover.

His mother emphatically did not want him to leave and became a real pain. His friends in Bloomsbury were not happy either, but slightly more understanding. Fellow novelist **Virginia Woolf**, 39, thinks she will never see him again; he will become a mystic and forget about his despised life back home in Weybridge. Besides the fact that she likes having him around, **Virginia** looks to Morgan's opinions on her writing. The rest of his Bloomsbury friends just think he's running away from home. Which he is.

Morgan did spend four idyllic hours in Port Said having sex on a chilly beach with his Egyptian lover.

But now that he is "away," what's he supposed to do?! Morgan knows that he doesn't have the skills necessary to organize the chaotic finances of the palace, and he isn't any better at supervising the gardens, the garages, or the electricity. He tried to start a literary society, but attendance was patchy and engagement by the participants non-existent. HH asked that Morgan read aloud to him every day; this happens maybe once a month.

Morgan should be using all his free time to write. He had planned to work on what he has called his "Indian Manuscript" which he had started before the Great War. Now he feels that the words on the page melt in the Indian humidity. All he is able to write are deceptively cheery letters back home.

The only bright spots are the instalments on royalties he is receiving from **Virginia's** Hogarth Press for his supernatural fiction, *The Story of the Siren;* the most recent was last month on the first anniversary of its publication. The fact that it has sold at all maybe means that he shouldn't give up trying to write.

# ❧ AUGUST 25, 1921 ❧
## THAME, OXFORDSHIRE, ENGLAND

It's a boy! Irish poet and playwright **William Butler Yeats**, 56, and his wife Georgie, 28, are over the moon about the birth of their second child, Michael Butler Yeats, now three days old.

*W. B. Yeats*

**Willie** had cabled his father, painter John Butler "JB" Yeats, 82, and their friend, Irish-American lawyer John Quinn, 51, both in New York City, as soon as he knew Michael and Georgie were okay. He doesn't mention the baby's name because he knows his Dad will be disappointed that the newest Yeats isn't named for him.

Today he is writing to Quinn that his son is "better looking than a newborn canary." And that he thinks his daughter, Anne, two, is flirting with him.

Before Michael's birth, Georgie's doctor had warned **Willie** that not all babies are as well behaved as their first, Anne. But the new Dad is so thrilled that it's a boy, he is not worried about any future behavior problems. He's just glad everyone is healthy.

Downstairs in their big house, Georgie is ushering in an "electrician"— actually a doctor. She has sworn the staff to secrecy about Michael's illness so **Willie** won't worry. She hopes he doesn't notice the maid who is crying.

*Spoiler alert: Michael overcame his illness and lived to a ripe old age. I met him in 2004.*

# ❧ LATE AUGUST, 1921 ❧
## 74 GLOUCESTER PLACE, MARYLEBONE, LONDON;
### AND SHAKESPEARE AND COMPANY,
### 12 RUE DE L'ODEON, PARIS

Harriet Shaw Weaver, 44, publisher of the *Egoist* magazine, founder of the Egoist Press, and benefactor of many novelists and poets, has come to a decision.

She has heard rumors that one of the writers she supports [well, at least one] uses the money she sends to regularly get drunk. Irish novelist James Joyce, 39, living in Paris, has written to assure her that these are just rumors. Although he does mention that he probably drinks a bit too much.

Weaver has decided that Joyce's bad habits are irrelevant in the face of his tremendous talent. Not only is she going to continue to support him, but also she is going to become his only publisher in the United Kingdom. For £15 she purchases the rights to his book of poetry published 14 years ago, *Chamber Music,* as well as, for £150, the copyrights to his early short story collection, *Dubliners,* and his play, *Exiles.*

Joyce has told her that American ex-patriate Sylvia Beach, 34, has offered to publish his novel-in-progress, *Ulysses,* through her Paris bookstore, Shakespeare and Company. Harriet is working with Sylvia to time the publication of the novel in England so that it doesn't hurt sales of Beach's publication in Paris.

Joyce assures both women that he's optimistic the novel could still be ready this fall.

In Paris, after Joyce collapses in a music hall from the strain of working 16 hours a day on his book, he decides to change his work habits.

Now he limits writing and revising *Ulysses* to five or six hours each day and spends more time on eight-mile walks around Paris.

His eye pain has become a bit more bearable, and he is working on 10 different episodes in the novel at the same time. Joyce has revised one section, "Aeolus," to incorporate headlines which weren't in any of the excerpts which appeared in the American magazine *The Little Review.* This changes the orientation of the second half of the book, which is already being sent off to a printer in Dijon to be set into galleys.

The printer comes back to Joyce with all kinds of questions. Why so many compound words? Those are usually two words. Are you sure you want them as one word? Only one of the men who works there has any grasp of the English language at all.

And Joyce and Beach are running out of typists. They have all given up in frustration over Joyce's handwritten color-coded insertions to be incorporated into the text.

*James Joyce's* Chamber Music

Recently they have enlisted an American drinking buddy of Joyce's, fellow novelist and sometimes publisher **Robert McAlmon**, 26. He is doing his best with the four notebooks full of changes marked in red, yellow, blue, purple and green in Joyce's scrawl.

For the first few pages of the all-important "Penelope" section, **McAlmon** is meticulous about determining exactly where Joyce means each phrase to go. He has even re-typed a whole page to make sure everything is in the right place.

But after a bit, **McAlmon** muses, does it really matter when the character Molly Bloom thinks this, that or the other? What difference does it make if those thoughts go here, or there, or a few pages later, or maybe not at all. So he just puts them in wherever he is typing.

He wonders if Joyce will notice.

*Robert McAlmon*

# ❧ AUGUST 31, 1921 ❧
## SCRIBNER'S, 153-157 FIFTH AVENUE, NEW YORK CITY, NEW YORK

S cribner's editor Maxwell Perkins, 36, knows that he has to be really upbeat and optimistic.

He has received a letter from his star author, **F. Scott Fitzgerald**, 24, whose second novel, *The Beautiful and Damned,* will be serialized in *Metropolitan* magazine next month. Scribner's predicts it will be as big a hit as his first, published last year, *This Side of Paradise.*

**Fitzgerald** is back home in St. Paul, Minnesota, where he and his wife, Zelda, 21, have moved to await the birth of their first child.

With the royalties from *Paradise,* the **Fitzgeralds** sailed to Europe earlier this year, but the trip was pretty disastrous as Zelda was sick the whole time.

*626 Goodrich Avenue, St. Paul, Minnesota*

Thanks to Perkins, they did meet with one of Scribner's older stars, English novelist John Galsworthy, 54, when they were in London. Perkins wrote to Galsworthy that their meeting "may turn out to have done **[Fitzgerald]** a great deal of good, for he needs steering."

Now Perkins is worried about the latest letter from **Scott**. He says that he has had a "hell of a time" trying to write again.

❝ Loafing puts me in this particular obnoxious and abominable gloom. My third novel, if I ever write another, will I am sure be black as death with gloom…I should like to sit down with half dozen chosen companions and drink myself to death but I am sick alike of life, liquor and literature. If it wasn't for Zelda I think I'd disappear out of sight for three years. Ship as a sailor or something & get hard—I'm sick of the flabby semi-intellectual softness in which I flounder with my generation."

Max puts as much enthusiasm as he can into his reply:

❝ Everybody that practices the last [literature] is at uncertain intervals weary of the first [life], but that is the very time they are likely to take strongly to the second [liquor]."

Perkins also extols the benefits of being in the St. Paul weather because **Scott** will want to stay inside and write most of the time.

# ❧ END OF SUMMER, 1921 ❧
## MIDTOWN MANHATTAN, NEW YORK CITY, NEW YORK

It's been an interesting summer in New York. The *Ziegfeld Follies of 1921* opened at Broadway's Globe Theatre, with music once again by Victor Herbert, 62. The leads are Fanny Brice, 29, coming back to the *Follies* after 10 years, singing "My Man" and "Second Hand Rose," and comedian and juggler W. C. Fields, 41, his fifth time in the *Follies*.

*Fanny Brice*

This was followed two weeks later by the premiere of *George White's Scandals* at the Liberty Theatre, a few blocks away from the Globe. The music is by George Gershwin, 22, who hit it big two years ago when Broadway star Al Jolson, 36, heard the composer sing his tune "Swanee" at a party and used it in one of his shows.

And just two days after that a new musical, *Dulcy,* by two young playwrights, both from western Pennsylvania, **Marc Connelly**, 30, and **George S Kaufman**, 31, opened just down 42nd Street at the Frazee Theatre. For their first collaboration, **Connelly** and **Kaufman** based the lead on a character in a *Tribune* column by one of their friends they lunch with regularly at the nearby Algonquin Hotel, **Franklin Pierce Adams**, 39, known to all of New York as **FPA**.

The duo has already started in on their next musical project, *To the Ladies!*, set to premiere next year.

One of their other lunch buddies, **Robert Benchley**, 31, an editor at the humor magazine *Life,* had finally gotten around to having his first drink while listening to the live broadcast of the Dempsey-Carpentier fight at the midtown speakeasy Tony Soma's. Soon after, **Benchley** tried some rye whiskey and realized it smelled just like his uncle did at family picnics back in Massachusetts.

**Benchley's** best friend, and now best drinking buddy, free-lance writer **Dorothy Parker**, just turned 28, has had another short story in the *Saturday Evening Post,* "An Apartment House Trilogy," based mostly on the characters around the flat she and her husband moved to just about a year ago, at 57 West 57th Street. When she sent the piece to the editor, she had warned him that it was "rotten…poisonous." He didn't think it was too rotten, but not quite her best. He really wants more of the shorter fluffy things she's been selling to **Benchley** over at *Life.*

**Bob** has introduced **Dottie** to one of his other friends, Donald Ogden Stewart, 26, who has had some pieces in *Vanity Fair* and *Smart Set.* He's been hanging out at **Parker's** place but doesn't like joining the others at their Algonquin lunches. They're vicious. Stewart feels he has to fortify himself with a few drinks before he even gets to the hotel.

Edna Ferber, just turned 36 [but only admits to 34], would love to be invited to one of the Algonquin lunches. Her second novel, *The Girls,* has just come out and it wasn't easy to get a national magazine to serialize it. Her story of unmarried Chicago women is too scandalous for most, but finally *Women's Home Companion* bought it without any major changes. Not only did **FPA** praise the way she described his hometown of Chicago, even her own mother conceded that it's not too bad.

Ferber has asked her friend **Alexander Woollcott**, 34, the *New York Times* drama critic, if she could lunch with him at the Algonquin maybe just once?

**Alex** took a leave of absence from his *Times* job this summer to go back to his alma mater, Hamilton College up in New York state, to finish a book he's been working on, *Mr. Dickens Goes to the Play.* He's written a few chapters about Charles Dickens' love of theatre and will fill out the rest with sections from Dickens' novels and essays.

But the biggest news in New York publishing this summer is how the new editor of the *New York World,* Herbert Bayard Swope, 39, has been stealing columnists from his competitors.

*Herbert Bayard Swope*

Swope became executive editor of the paper last year and has been making big changes. He thought the page opposite the editorials was a mess, so he cleared out the book reviews and obituaries and now devotes the page to opinion pieces, christening it the "op-ed" page. Swope believes,

> "Nothing is more interesting than opinion when opinion is interesting."

Those pesky facts can stay where they belong in the rest of the paper.

Swope stole one of the top columnists at the *Tribune,* **Heywood Broun**, 32, another regular Algonquin luncher. **Broun** was eager to jump. Swope makes clear to him and all his columnists that they can write whatever they want—within the limits of libel law and good taste. In return, they have to create new copy for each instalment, three times a week. No hoarding a bank of evergreen filler, ready to print any time. Swope wants it all to be fresh.

For $25,000 a year, in his column "It Seems to Me" on the op-ed page, **Broun** has great freedom. He can write theatre reviews, report on the most recent football game of his alma mater, Harvard, or campaign about social issues such as censorship, racial discrimination or academic freedom.

*Heywood Broun*

Poaching **Broun** is a coup. But Swope astounds New York's literati again by luring the *Tribune's* number one columnist, **FPA** himself, over to the *World*. Unlike the other writers, **FPA** is given his own private office to work on his "Conning Tower" columns. One of the first is about the return to New York City of his fellow Algonquin-ite, **Alex Woollcott**.

Maybe **Woollcott** will be the next star to jump ship and land on Swope's *World*?

*There is a recent article about how digital media has affected the "op-ed" page here. https://www.quickanddirtytips.com/education/grammar/what-does-op-ed-mean?e=896500ae5775abb f55132666dc4ff1b135276bf340a7e2fbaaccf3694fae62bb*

# ✺ SEPTEMBER 6, 1921 ✺
## ROOM 1219, ST. FRANCIS HOTEL,
### CORNER OF GEARY AND POWELL STREETS,
### SAN FRANCISCO, CALIFORNIA

Roscoe Arbuckle, 34, is waking up in this posh hotel room and slowly starting to remember what a disaster last night's party had been.

His butt is still sore from a stupid accident back home in Los Angeles a few days ago when he sat on some rags soaked in acid that burnt through his pants causing second degree burns.

But Roscoe's friends insisted that he come with them anyway for this planned Labor Day weekend bash to celebrate the hit films Roscoe starred in this year—and his new $1 million contract with Paramount. One of the

*Virginia Rappe*

guys bought him a rubber padded ring to sit on for the long drive.

The suite in this hotel—two bedrooms for them and a party room for everyone—along with the women and the booze have all been arranged by his friends.

Roscoe is familiar with two of the women from Hollywood. Virginia Rappe, 26, is an actress and sometimes model who was in a film a few years ago with Rudolph Valentino, also 26. Since then Valentino has become quite a star based on his most recent picture, *The Four Horsemen of the Apocalypse*. But Virginia has only done bit parts and is mostly known for getting drunk and vomiting at every party.

Her friend, Maud Delmont, 35, has an even more scandalous reputation. She provides young women for wealthy men who are then accused of rape and blackmailed. Delmont has even been convicted of fraud and extortion.

Roscoe was a bit concerned when he first saw those two in the suite yesterday morning. If the local cops find out, they might feel they have to look into this illegal liquor party.

Yesterday afternoon he found Virginia in his bathroom, vomiting, as usual. He carried her into his room.

*Maude Delmont*

But a bit later, Virginia was on the floor, screaming and ripping at her clothes. Other guests tried to cool her down in a tub of cold water. Roscoe called the hotel manager and doctor, who decided that the young woman had just had too much to drink and could sleep it off. The doctor gave her some morphine.

Roscoe figures he'd better get up now and see how she and the others are doing. Virginia was pretty sick last night.

From the other room he hears one of his friends call him,

❝ Hey, Fatty…"

Disgusted, Roscoe yells back,

❝ I have a name, y'know.

# ❧ SEPTEMBER, 1921 ❧
## CENTRAL PARK WEST, NEW YORK CITY, NEW YORK

He is still fuming. A few days ago, lawyer and art collector John Quinn, 51, was quoted in the *New York Times* calling the protest against the Metropolitan Museum of Art's first exhibit of modern French painting, "Ku Klux criticism." He meant it. Still does.

Even the *Times* can't determine who is behind the four-page pamphlet,

66  A Protest Against the Present Exhibit of Degenerate 'Modernistic' Works in the Metropolitan Museum of Art [by] An Anonymous Committee of Citizens and Supporters"

Here's what these self-appointed critics have to say:

66  This 'Modernistic' degenerate cult is simply the Bolshevic philosophy applied to art...*The real cult of 'Modernism' began with a small group of neurotic Ego-Maniacs in Paris who styled themselves "Satanists"—worshippers of Satan—the God of Ugliness*...It is understandable that the Museum should decide, in the interest of public Enlightenment, to lend its galleries for the Exhibition of such Art Monstrocities [sic] in order to give the public an opportunity to see...specimens of so-called 'Art' which has been boosted into notoriety in Europe and now here, by the most vulgar, crafty and brazen methods of advertisement by the European speculators in Art...[But] the Trustees should publicly...disclaim all intention of lending the prestige of the Museum in support of the propaganda for Bolshevistic Art, which is repudiated by the majority of our artists and citizens."

This is Quinn's own collection they are criticizing. He has lent 26 pieces to the show—modestly titled "Loan Exhibition of Impressionist and Post-Impressionist Paintings"—including Cezanne's *Madame Cezanne in a*

*Red Armchair* and Van Gogh's *Portrait of the Artist.* One of his fellow collectors has even told Quinn how jealous he is of his pieces in the exhibit.

The American *Art News* gave the exhibit a positive review when it opened back in May. But the *New York World* called it "dangerous" and singled out one of Quinn's Gauguins as an "odious Bolshevik work."

*Lilly P. Bliss*

Quinn and Lilly P. Bliss, 57, along with some other New York patrons, negotiated with the Museum to host this show, and Quinn thinks that, if anything, it is too conservative. They have included Spanish painter Pablo Picasso, 39, for example, but none of his Cubist work.

Quinn and Bliss have collaborated before, to introduce the American public to contemporary art at The Armory Show. It was a huge success. But eight years later self-righteous Philistines are still protesting in print.

This summer the Museum hosted a solo show of drawings by a woman! Is anyone protesting *that?*, Quinn asks.

# ❧ MID-SEPTEMBER, 1921 ❧
## 1239 NORTH DEARBORN STREET, CHICAGO, ILLINOIS

Newlyweds **Ernest**, 22, and Hadley **Hemingway**, 29, have just returned to their cramped, gloomy, top floor walk-up apartment after a wonderful dinner with one of **Ernest's** mentors, novelist **Sherwood Anderson**, just turning 45.

**Anderson** represents the type of successful writer **Ernie** aspires to be. Two years ago **Sherwood's** novel—really a collection of interwoven stories about one town, *Winesburg, Ohio*—was a big hit. Since then two short story collections have been big sellers as well. The most recent, *The Triumph of the Egg: A Book of Impressions from American Life in Tales and Poems,* includes 15 stories and seven photos of clay sculptures by **Anderson's** wife, Tennessee Mitchell Anderson, 47, illustrating some of the characters.

**Anderson** is regularly published in *The Dial* literary magazine, where **Hemingway** regularly has his poems rejected.

**Sherwood** and Tennessee have just returned from their first trip to Europe and are filled with stories of the interesting people—mostly Americans— whom they became friends with there.

**Ernest** and Hadley are planning a trip to Europe also. But they want to move there permanently.

**Ernie** is making $200 a month as editor of the house organ for the Cooperative Commonwealth Society. But he is growing more suspicious of the organization every day. In addition to writing sections such as the Co-Op Notes, Personal Mentions and Insurance Notes in the newsletter, he's been including coverage of the allegations of fraud brought against the Society.

Hadley, on the other hand, has a bit of a trust fund. And with the recent death of an uncle she never cared much for anyway, she will soon have an income of almost $300 a month.

**Ernie** knows he can count on the *Toronto Star* to continue to pay him for free-lance pieces, and he wants to show Hadley the places he was in Italy during the Great War. Including where he was injured. They have even bought some lira—at a great exchange rate—in preparation for their trip.

But **Sherwood** has a different idea. Forget Italy, he tells the young couple. France is equally inexpensive and the most interesting writers and artists of the time are flocking there.

**Sherwood** promises **Ernest** he will write letters of introduction for him so he can meet **Anderson's** ex-pat American friends on the Left Bank. Sylvia Beach, 34, from Princeton, New Jersey, runs

*Hadley and Ernest Hemingway*

a terrific English-language bookshop. Even more important, the modernist writer **Gertrude Stein**, 47, from San Francisco [via Pittsburgh]. **Sherwood** has been a big fan of her work for years and was thrilled to have long discussions with her about writing. He is contributing the preface to a major anthology of her pieces from the past decade, *Geography and Plays,* in hopes of getting her a wider American audience.

Back here in their depressing apartment, the **Hemingways** are re-thinking their plans. **Anderson** has convinced them.

Let's go to Paris!

# ❧ SEPTEMBER 18, 1921 ❧
## EN ROUTE FROM TAORMINA, SICILY,
## TO FLORENCE, ITALY

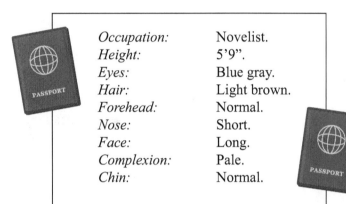

| | |
|---|---|
| *Occupation:* | Novelist. |
| *Height:* | 5'9". |
| *Eyes:* | Blue gray. |
| *Hair:* | Light brown. |
| *Forehead:* | Normal. |
| *Nose:* | Short. |
| *Face:* | Long. |
| *Complexion:* | Pale. |
| *Chin:* | Normal. |

That's how the British Foreign Office in London described Nottingham native David Herbert Lawrence, just turned 36, on the passport they issued him two years ago.

Now he is traveling from his current home in Sicily to the British consulate in Florence to get a renewal. He and his wife Frieda, 42, are feeling as though it may be time to move on.

They have been living in a beautiful hilltop home, Fontana Vecchia, since last year. They left England during the Great War, feeling as though Frieda's German nationality and David's supposedly "obscene" writings were not welcome.

After traveling around Europe, David managed to finish his most recent novel, *Aaron's Rod,* a few months ago, although it won't be published until next year. His UK publisher, after much waffling, finally brought out his *Women in Love* this past summer, to many negative reviews.

Lawrence has a travel piece coming out next month in *The Dial* magazine, but he hasn't been writing much. Except letters to his New York publisher:

> " I wish I could find a ship that would carry me round the world and land me somewhere in the West—New Mexico or California—and I could have a little house and two goats, somewhere away by myself."

With only about £40 in their British bank account, where can he and Frieda go? Maybe somewhere on a tramp steamer.

*D. H. Lawrence passport photo*

Friends are moving to Ceylon to study Buddhism, but the Lawrences have turned down their offer to join them.

David is still waiting to hear from his American agent about the current balance in his accounts there. Maybe that's the next option.

# ❧ SEPTEMBER 22, 1921 ❧
## SHAKESPEARE AND COMPANY,
## 12 RUE DE L'ODEON, PARIS

Which is worse: Financial problems or visiting family members? That's what is confronting ex-pat bookstore owner Sylvia Beach, 34, who is writing to her sister, Holly Beach Dennis, 37, in Italy to ask for money.

Sylvia and her partner, Adrienne Monnier, 29, who owns a French-language bookstore across the street, have just returned from a lovely holiday in Hyeres on the southeastern coast of France.

Now that they are back home Sylvia has to face her mother, here on her annual visit, joined by Mom's brother and his son.

In addition, the bill for renovations Sylvia had to have done to move her shop, Shakespeare and Company, to this new—much improved—location has come due. A total of 2,120Fr, including printing the announcement of the relocation.

But the bill that worries Sylvia the most is the one from the printer, Darantiere, in Dijon. He needs 1,000Fr for the work he has done setting type for *Ulysses,* the controversial novel by Irish ex-pat James Joyce, 39, which Sylvia has offered to publish. Darantiere has agreed to be paid in instalments, and Sylvia has solicited quite a few pre-orders from around the world. But not enough subscribers have sent checks yet to cover the growing expenses.

Reluctantly, Sylvia writes to Holly:

❝ I'm asking you to lend me a thousand francs!!! My carpentry bill will be handed in any day now and mother who was going to lend me all the money for my moving expenses had to stop off in the midst, having had a great deal of expense getting [their sister] Cyprian equipped as a rising film star…My business is going well [but I] have to put every single centime aside to pay the printer."

The plan is still to bring out *Ulysses* this fall, but Sylvia is dubious.

# ❧ LATE SEPTEMBER, 1921
## MONK'S HOUSE, RODMELL, ENGLAND

**❝** Oh, what a damned bore!"

**V**irginia Woolf, 39, wrote to a friend this past summer. She had been ill—and not working—for so long.

But now that it is autumn, with lovely weather and long walks out here in the countryside, she is

*Monk's House, Rodmell*

feeling better, and writing better than before.

**Virginia** and her husband, **Leonard**, 40, recently bought a used platen machine for their expanding Hogarth Press, which they run out of their London home. **Virginia's** short story collection, *Monday or Tuesday,* which they published earlier this year, is selling well. And she is now close to finishing her next novel, *Jacob's Room.*

One of many interruptions this month was the visit this past weekend of their friend, poet Tom Eliot, just turning 33. **Virginia** hadn't been looking forward to it. She wrote to her sister, painter **Vanessa Bell**, 42,

**❝** I suppose you wdn't come for the 24th? When Eliot will be here?"

But **Vanessa** wasn't available.

His stay turned out to be uneventful. Lots of chat about writing and books. **Virginia** confides in her diary that Tom's visit

    ❝   passed off successfully…& yet I am so disappointed to find that I am no longer afraid of him—"

꧁ ꧂

*Vivien Eliot*

Eliot hadn't mentioned this to the **Woolfs** this past weekend, but he is looking forward to a visit to a London nerve specialist. His wife, Vivien, 33, has made the appointment for him, because they have both agreed that his job at Lloyds Bank, a summer visit from his American family, and his work on a major poem, are all affecting his health, physical and mental. They may be moving out of hectic London soon, and are hoping that an upcoming trip to Paris to visit fellow poet, ex-pat American Ezra Pound, 35, might help. He and Pound are going to work together on editing Eliot's poem.

Vivien writes to one of their friends, jokingly, that she is seeking help for Tom but hasn't "nearly finished my own nervous breakdown yet."

Vivien has written a much longer letter to her brother-in-law, archaeologist Henry Ware Eliot, 41, just gone back home to St. Louis. Not joking, she confides that she knows her husband is not in love with her anymore. And Vivien adds a postscript,

    ❝   Good-bye Henry…And *be personal,* you must be personal, or else it's no good. Nothing's any good."

# ❧ SEPTEMBER 30, 1921 ❧
## SHILLINGFORD, BERKSHIRE, ENGLAND

Poet, playwright and new dad **William Butler Yeats**, 56, is writing to his friend in New York City, lawyer and art collector John Quinn, 51. **Yeats** and his wife, Georgie, 28, have just returned from taking their baby son, Michael Butler, one month old, to Dublin for an operation. All went well; however Michael might need more surgery, in London, next month.

But the **Yeatses** arrived home to find out that, once again, his father, painter John Butler "JB" **Yeats**, 82, has cancelled his booking to sail back home to his family in Ireland. This time he blames it on some recent sickness.

Both **Willie** and Quinn have virtually ordered JB to come home. Quinn is resenting taking care of the older man, and Yeats has told his father point blank that, with his growing family, he can no longer afford to support his Dad's American lifestyle.

Quinn has booked JB to sail in November and has put down a deposit. Again.

# ❧ OCTOBER, 1921 ❧
## HOTEL LA MAISON BLANCHE, 3 TRAVERSE DES LICES, SAINT TROPEZ, FRANCE

The friends from London's Bloomsbury neighborhood are settling in to this hotel on the French Riviera.

As soon as painter **Vanessa Bell**, 42, arrives, she writes to their friend, economist **John Maynard Keynes**, 38, back home, asking him to send them a dozen packages of oatmeal, 10 seven-pound tins of marmalade, four pounds of tea, and "some potted meat."

Vanessa is here with her former lover, art critic **Roger Fry**, 54, who has received a letter from **Vanessa's** sister, novelist **Virginia**

*Hotel La Maison Blanche*

**Woolf**, 39, reporting on a recent evening at her country home in Sussex:

> ❝ T. S. Eliot says that [James Joyce's novel *Ulysses*] is the greatest work of the age—**Lytton [Strachey]** says he doesn't mean to read it. **Clive [Bell, Vanessa's** estranged husband] says—well, **Clive** says that [his mistress] Mary Hutchinson has a dressmaker who would make me look like other people."

Also here for the winter is **Vanessa's** partner, painter **Duncan Grant**, 36, who has arrived via Paris.

Visitors or not, **Vanessa** intends to spend her time here working on still lifes and interiors, in preparation for her first solo show next spring.

# ❧ OCTOBER 7, 1921 ❧

## 1239 NORTH DEARBORN STREET, CHICAGO, ILLINOIS

The Cooperative Society of America has officially been put into receivership. To no one's surprise.

And the least surprised is the editor of their newsletter, *Cooperative Commonwealth,* newly married would-be novelist **Ernest Hemingway**, 22.

The founders and executives of the Society are accused of fraud for selling "beneficial interest certificates" to farmers, widows, and small businessmen for half down and half in instalments. But $11 million of the capital went into paper companies and the treasurer has taken off to Canada with about $3 million.

*Chicago street*

The judge has turned the evidence over to a grand jury.

*Paris street*

**Ernie** is at home, reading the *Chicago Tribune's* coverage of the story. He knows that he has to write about it too, in the organization's own newsletter.

And start packing to move to Paris with his new wife.

# ❧ EARLY OCTOBER, 1921 ❧
## HOTEL ALBEMARLE, 47 EASTERN ESPLANADE, MARGATE, KENT, ENGLAND

This could work. American ex-patriate poet, Tom Eliot, 33, and his wife, Vivien, also 33, are settling in for a three-week stay here in Cliftonville, a bit more than 60 miles northeast of London, during one of the hottest Octobers on record.

Tom has found a Victorian shed, the Nayland Rock Shelter, near the shore on Margate sands, that he can commute to each day by tram from Cliftonville. This will give him the seclusion he needs to work on the epic poem he has been trying to write since he moved to England more than seven years ago.

This beats the commute that he has been doing every workday to his job at Lloyds Bank by Moorgate station in noisy east London from their Clarence Gate Gardens apartment in Marylebone. He enjoys the commute; but not the job.

His job, combined with a two-month visit from his American family, and his insistence on trying to write this poem are taking their toll. Last month, Vivien arranged for Tom to be examined by one of the most celebrated nerve specialists in the country. The doctor strongly recommended that Eliot take two to three months off from everything. And everybody. Including Vivien. But she insisted on coming here with him.

The reputation of the doctor was the deciding factor. Lloyds agreed on the first of this month to grant Tom a three-month leave of absence, with full pay, to begin as soon as he trained his replacement, which he did last week.

Vivien is happy to be quit of London, describing their last night there with friends as

  ❝   *What* a last impression of London…the monotony, the *drivel* of the whole stupid round."

Now that they are in Margate, Tom is already eating better. And looking forward to commuting to his beach shed each day to work on his as yet untitled poem. Vivien is planning to write to Scofield Thayer, 31, the editor of the American literary magazine *The Dial,* explaining that Tom will not be able to submit any more of

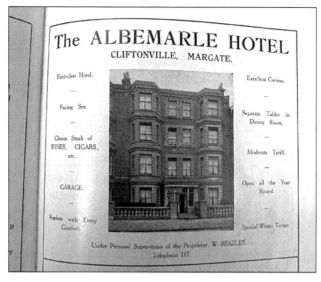

The **ALBEMARLE** HOTEL
CLIFTONVILLE, MARGATE.

First-class Hotel.

Facing Sea.

Choice Stock of WINES, CIGARS, etc.

GARAGE.

Replete with Every Comfort.

Excellent Cuisine.

Separate Tables in Dining Room.

Moderate Tariff.

Open all the Year Round.

Special Winter Terms

Under Personal Supervision of the Proprietor, W. BEAZLEY.
Telephone 117.

*Ad for Hotel Albemarle*

his "London Letter" essays to the magazine until January at least.

But what will happen after their three-week stay here?

Tom is planning to take a holiday in Paris and bring along the "hoard of fragments" as he refers to the pencil scrawlings that are now the poem, to work on there with his fellow American friend and mentor, Ezra Pound, 35.

In addition, Viv has received advice from a friend of theirs who also suffers from depression, socialite and hostess, Lady Ottoline Morrell, 48. She has told them that the sickness leaves her

66 utterly dead & empty & it is like being in a cold fog—or a pond."

Ottoline has recommended a doctor in Switzerland who treated her brother.

Vivien wants Tom to go there after a few days in Paris.

Down in London, after much debate, Parliament has voted to return to the longer pub hours in force before the Great War, pleasing the pub owners but not the moral guardians of society.

And to emphasize the importance of Remembrance Day, the anniversary of the signing of the Armistice, November 11, Field Marshall Douglas Haig, 60, has proposed declaring it Poppy Day. Citizens throughout the country will make their patriotism visible to all by wearing bright red poppies in their lapels.

# ❧ FALL, 1921 ❧
## NEW YORK CITY; AND ROME

*The New York Times Magazine* features an interview with comedian Charlie Chaplin, 32, with the first byline by the *Times'* first woman full-time writer, Jane Grant, 29. She and her husband, **Harold Ross**, just turning 29, are living on her salary, and saving his earnings as editor of *Judge,* to bankroll a magazine they want to start.

At the *New York World,* Herbert Bayard Swope, 39, who took over as executive editor last year, is running front page articles 21 straight days in a row, exposing the Ku Klux Klan as a white supremacist organization. the *World's* investigation reveals that not only is the KKK terrorizing Blacks, Jews and immigrants, they are also harassing Catholics in the courts. The KKK is suing all the papers that carry the *World's* series.

*Ad in the* New York Tribune *placed by the* New York World

Down in Greenwich Village, the autumn issue of *The Little Review,* recently convicted of publishing obscene material, proclaims:

> ❝ As protest against the suppression of *The Little Review,* containing various instalments of the *Ulysses* of James Joyce, the following artists and writers of international reputation are collaborating in the autumn number of *Little Review.*"

The list includes the magazine's foreign editor, American ex-pat poet Ezra Pound, 35, and writer and artist Jean Cocteau, 32. On the last page the magazine announces that, because *Ulysses* is to be published soon as a book in Paris,

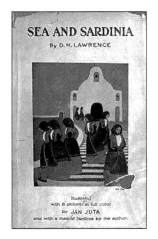

Sea and Sardinia *by D. H. Lawrence*

 We limp from the field."

The most recent issue of *The Dial* magazine contains an excerpt from *Sea and Sardinia,* by D. H. Lawrence, just turned 36. He complains to his agent that the magazine edited his piece of travel writing so that it is "very much cut up… Damn them for that."

In Rome, Harold Loeb, just turning 30, and Alfred Kreymborg, 38, have produced the first issue of a new magazine, *Broom, i*ncluding work by two of their fellow Americans: A short story by **Sherwood Anderson**, just turning 45, and *Sequidilla* by **Man Ray**, 31. To choose a title, the founders came up with a list of one-syllable words and randomly chose "broom." *Broom* is dedicated to giving "the unknown, path-breaking artist" the opportunity to sweep away their predecessors. But Loeb feels that this first issue has too many predecessors and not enough unknowns.

# ❧ MID-OCTOBER, 1921 ❧
## SHAKESPEARE AND COMPANY,
## 12 RUE DE L'ODEON, PARIS; NEW YORK CITY

Well, she lost that bet. American ex-patriate Sylvia Beach, 34, owner of this bookstore, had sent a subscription form to legendary Irish playwright, George Bernard Shaw, 65, in London. His former secretary had assured Sylvia that the irascible old man is quite generous. Sylvia kindly asked him if he would like to subscribe in advance for one of the deluxe editions of the novel, *Ulysses,* by his countryman James Joyce, 39, which she is planning to publish this fall.

Joyce has never liked Shaw, referring to him as "a born preacher." He warned Sylvia that the answer will be no. So they bet on it. A silk handkerchief for Beach if Shaw says yes; a box of Voltigeur cigars for Joyce if Shaw says no.

Today she receives a letter saying that *Ulysses,* which Shaw has read excerpts of in the *Egoist* magazine, is

❝ a revolting record of a disgusting phase of civilization…but a truthful one. [Beach must be] a young barbarian beglamored by the excitements and enthusiasms that art stirs up in passionate material, but to me…it is all hideously real."

Shaw compares Joyce's work to making "a cat cleanly by rubbing its nose in its own filth."

He ends by saying,

❝ I am an elderly Irish gentleman,..If you imagine that any Irishman, much less an elderly one, would pay 150Fr for a book, you little know my countrymen."

Sylvia pays up to Joyce.

✕

To raise more money for the publication of *Ulysses,* and the support of Joyce, Sylvia has written once again to one of his patrons, Irish-American attorney John Quinn, 51, pleading,

❝ I give him everything I can spare but as you may imagine my shop has not been in existence long enough to support [Joyce's] family of four people as well as myself…It is up to all of us who want the most important book of today to appear to come to the help of its author."

This only angers Quinn, so he checks with another of Joyce's benefactors, American poet Ezra Pound, 35, now living in London. Quinn says he'll send the money if Pound thinks Joyce really needs it, but

❝ I'll be damned if I'll do it because Miss Beach asks for it."

Pound assures him that Joyce isn't starving. Quinn doesn't send the money.

# ❧ OCTOBER 20, 1921 ❧
## VIENNA, AUSTRIA

Scofield Thayer, 31, editor of the American literary magazine, *The Dial,* has come here specifically to be psychoanalysed by the legendary Professor Sigmund Freud, 65, for a fee of $100 per week.

On the way from New York City to Vienna, Thayer stopped off for a bit in Paris, meeting up with one of his magazine's main contributors, American ex-pat poet Ezra Pound, about to turn 36, who was kind enough to introduce him around to other ex-pats such as writer **Gertrude Stein**, 47, and her partner **Alice B. Toklas**, 44.

With him in Paris was yet another American poet, E. E. Cummings, just turned 27. Thayer has been helping to raise the daughter Cummings fathered two years ago with Thayer's wife, Elaine Orr Thayer, 25.

*Sigmund Freud*

Scofield and Elaine have just recently finalized their divorce.

While Scofield is living in Vienna, which he plans will be for the next two years, he is still running *The Dial*. He supervises the contents, approves layouts, and tries to drum up some investment from wealthy Europeans he knows.

Thayer has decided to abandon his European expansion plans for his magazine. Another of his ex-pat American contributors, Tom Eliot, 33, and he have been in talks with Lady Margaret Rothermere, 47, wife of the publisher of the UK's *Daily Mail* newspaper, about funding a UK version of *The Dial*.

But it has become clear that Lady Rothermere is more interested in supporting a new magazine that Eliot has proposed—*The Criterion*—rather than the expansion of an existing one from the States.

Withdrawing from the field, today Thayer writes to Eliot's wife Vivien, 33, who is now handling all of Tom's correspondence, that "the multiplication of magazines" in the market would not be a good thing:

❝ The more artistic journals you publish the more money is wasted on printers, and paper dealers and the less is left for the artists themselves."

# ✖ LATE OCTOBER, 1921 ✖

## SHAKESPEARE AND COMPANY,
## 12 RUE DE L'ODEON, PARIS

Irish novelist James Joyce, 39, is doing his best to get his *Ulysses* finished in time for a promised November publication. Actually, it was a promised October publication, but they missed that.

His publisher, American ex-pat bookstore owner, Sylvia Beach, 34, is dealing with angry subscribers who were expecting to have copies in hand by now. British army officer T. E. Lawrence, 33, is particularly mad as he has ordered two of the expensive deluxe copies.

But Sylvia figures that, as she hasn't yet accepted any money from the subscribers, she isn't cheating anyone.

Joyce is working hard, not only writing but also correcting proofs received back from the printer. He writes to a friend that the typesetters are

*T. E. Lawrence*

66    boggled by all the w's and k's in our tongue and can do only about
     100 pages at a time...However, I am doing my best to push [Stephen]
     Bloom on to the stage of the world."

Sylvia and the printer are also having a hard time finding the cover paper Joyce wants, the same blue as the Greek flag.

As he writes and revises, Joyce keeps expanding the text, by as much as 20%.

At the same time, he is also working with one of his French friends, writer Valery Larbaud, 40, on a French translation of the novel. In the backroom of another Left Bank bookshop, La Maison des Amis des Livres, owned by Sylvia's partner, Adrienne Monnier, 29, Joyce is getting help with the translation from a young music student. Bilingual Jacques Benoist Mechin, 20, has also made some good suggestions, particularly about the ending. Joyce wanted to finish Molly Bloom's soliloquy with "I will." But he likes Mechin's idea of ending with "Yes."

# ❧ MIDNIGHT ❧
# OCTOBER 29/30, 1921
## 9 RUE DE L'UNIVERSITE, PARIS

Irish novelist James Joyce, 39, writes,

" Trieste-Zurich-Paris, 1914-1921,"

and puts down his pen.

*Ulysses* is finished.

# ✖ EARLY NOVEMBER, 1921 ✖
## CORSO UMBERTO, TOARMINA, SICILY

Walking back to his rented house, Fontana Vecchia, British ex-pat novelist David Herbert Lawrence, 36, is casually sorting through the mail he just picked up at the local post office.

There is an unusual smell.

Not a bad smell. An exotic, Indian smell.

It's coming from an envelope that has in it, not a letter, but a long scroll. Like a papyrus. From the United States. From a city in New Mexico called "Taos."

As he walks, Lawrence unfurls the scroll and starts reading. He stops in his tracks.

This unusual package is from an American woman he has never heard of, Mabel Dodge Sterne, 42. She has included a few leaves of local plants, desachev and osha, to entice Lawrence to accept her invitation to move to Taos and live rent-free on her land. And write.

Lawrence can't believe what he is reading.

Sterne has seen an excerpt of his upcoming travel book, *Sea and Sardinia,* in last month's issue of *The Dial*

*Mabel Dodge*

magazine, and she is impressed. She likes the "queer way…[he gives] the feel and touch and smell of places."

She wants him to write about Taos in the same way and is offering him an adobe cottage, filled with furniture handmade in the area, with room enough for his wife and children. Well, if he has any children. [He doesn't.]

This is exactly the opportunity Lawrence and his wife, Frieda, 42, are looking for. They considered joining some friends who are going to study Buddhism in Ceylon. But this—this. Financial as well as emotional support.

As he heads home to tell Frieda, he nibbles at the osha. It tastes like liquorice and takes him far away from the tacky shops lining the Corso Umberto.

Lawrence can think of a hundred questions he has to ask.

Who is this woman? He will write to his New York agent to find out if he has ever heard of Mrs. Sterne.

Where is this Taos? He will try to find it on a map.

Then he will write back to Mabel with an enthusiastic

❝ Yes!"

Followed by his other questions: Are there trees? Water?! Maybe a river or a lake. Is it hot or cold there? What type of clothing should they bring?

Lawrence also thinks he needs to assure Mrs. Sterne that he and Frieda will eventually pay rent to her. He doesn't want to spend the rest of his life being as poor as he has been so far. Writing all these books should pay off some time.

# ❧ EARLY NOVEMBER, 1921 ❧
## 9 RUE DE L'UNIVERSITE PARIS

Fresh from the achievement of having finished his novel *Ulysses* at the end of last month, Irish ex-pat James Joyce, 39, wrote a few days ago to one of his English benefactors, Harriet Shaw Weaver, 45, in London:

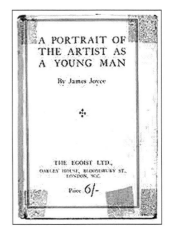

A Portrait of the Artist as a Young Man *published by The Egoist Press*

❝ A coincidence is that of birthdays in connection with my books. *A Portrait of the Artist as a Young Man* which first appeared serially in your paper [*The Egoist* magazine] on 2 February [his birthday] finished on 1 September [her birthday]. *Ulysses* began on 1 March (birthday. of a friend of mine, a Cornish painter) and was finished on Mr. [Ezra] Pound's birthday [30 October], he tells me. I wonder on whose it will be published?"

Now Joyce is wondering. What about February?

# ❧ NOVEMBER 8, 1921 ❧
## NEW YORK CITY, NEW YORK

Famous Players-Lasky Pictures has a hit on their hands. *The Sheik,* starring Rudolph Valentino, 26, opened in Los Angeles a bit more than a week ago and audiences love it. Critics have their doubts. Some feel the film shouldn't have left out the key rape scene that was in the original British novel.

But Jesse Lasky, 41, founder of the studio, feels that the film does justice to the novel and sensitive scenes were handled well.

He's pleased with Valentino, who is already popular from his earlier films, particularly *The Four Horsemen of the Apocalypse* which was released this spring by Metro Pictures.

*Poster for Jesse Lasky presents* The Sheik

Metro didn't treat Valentino well, and Lasky has lured him to Famous Players.

*The Sheik* opened here in New York City two days ago, and is breaking attendance records at two major theatres, the Rialto and the Rivoli, among others.

Lasky feels that when the film is released nationwide in two weeks, there will be a similar response. He's thinking of promotional ideas to push it even more. Like maybe, "Sheik Week."

He prefers to spend his time coming up with ideas like this, rather than thinking about the charges the U. S. Federal Trade Commission is bringing against his company for intimidating theatre owners into block booking films.

# ❧ NOVEMBER 11, 1921 ❧
## ARLINGTON NATIONAL CEMETERY,
## ARLINGTON COUNTY, VIRGINIA;
## AND WESTMINSTER ABBEY, LONDON

Just across the Potomac River from Washington D. C., the first entombment of an American "unknown soldier" is taking place to commemorate the third Armistice Day, the anniversary of the end of the Great War.

Chosen randomly by a U. S. Army sergeant from four sets of remains taken from four cemeteries on the French battlefields, this soldier has literally had a stormy journey to get here.

*Armistice Day ceremony*

On its way to France to collect the precious cargo, the *USS Olympia* was hit by a tropical storm in the Atlantic.

On the way back, the weather was even worse. The ship took on water and the Marine Guard assigned to the casket was almost washed overboard. Hit again by the same tropical storm, the *Olympia* sustained 13-foot waves.

But the remains arrived safely. Speaking at the ceremony, President Warren G. Harding, 56, remarks,

**" "** We know not whence he came, only that his death marks him with the everlasting glory of an American dying for his country."

🙘🙚

In London, this is the third year that the United Kingdom has commemorated Remembrance Day.

Last year the UK government, along with the government of their ally, France, buried remains of an "unknown warrior" and a *"soldat inconnu."*

Lord Field Marshall Haig, 60, who commanded the British Expeditionary Force, has felt that the country's reverence for the importance of the day is already waning. He proposed asking his countrymen to remember those who are buried under the poppies in Flanders Field by buying and wearing commemorative poppies. And shaming those who don't.

*Poppy pin*

The first Poppy Day appears to be a success. They are on track for sales of eight million poppy pins.

*Poppy Day continues to this day: https://en.wikipedia.org/wiki/Remembrance_Day*

# ❧ EARLY NOVEMBER, 1921 ❧
## SCRIBNER'S, 153-157 FIFTH AVENUE,
## NEW YORK CITY, NEW YORK;
## AND 626 GOODRICH AVENUE, ST. PAUL, MINNESOTA

Throughout the fall, Scribner's editor Maxwell Perkins, 37, has been corresponding with his star author, **F. Scott Fitzgerald**, 25, currently back in his hometown of St. Paul with his wife Zelda, 21.

**Scott** dropped off the completed manuscript of his second novel, *The Beautiful and Damned,* at the end of April and headed off to London and Paris with a pregnant Zelda.

Last month **Fitzgerald,** like most authors, complained to Max about the minimal advertising for his first novel, last year's hit *This Side of Paradise.* Perkins encouraged him to express any of his dissatisfactions and to keep sending suggestions. He assured **Scott** that

❝ the more you help us in connection with the make-up of these advertisements, the better. I think we did more advertising, very probably, than you were aware of, but it was not as effective or as plainly visible as it should have been. But we have now a man with excellent experience whom we believe will do the work with skill and vigor...I only want to ask you always to criticize freely....and to convince you that, in the case of *The Beautiful and Damned,* we will work the scheme out with you so that...you will feel satisfaction both with the copy and the campaign."

Of course, say what you will about the advertising, *Paradise* was Scribner's biggest success last year.

Then, while **Scott** was correcting page proofs, he asked Perkins for some help with details about student life at Harvard that he wanted to include.

Having graduated from there in 1907 with a degree in economics, Perkins was happy to oblige.

Last month, the editor was also pleased to pass on to **Fitzgerald** that he had seen one of the stenographers

> taking some proofs out to lunch with her...because she could not stop reading it. That is the way with all of them who are near enough to get their hands on the proofs—not only the stenographers."

Two years ago, Perkins had to fight the Scribner's editorial board to have them publish a novel as different as *Paradise*. Now the whole house is anticipating that they have another hit on their hands with *The Beautiful and Damned*.

Today Max is writing **Scott** an even cheerier letter, congratulating him on the birth of his daughter, Frances Scott Fitzgerald, one week old. When "Scottie" was born, **Scott** telegraphed his parents,

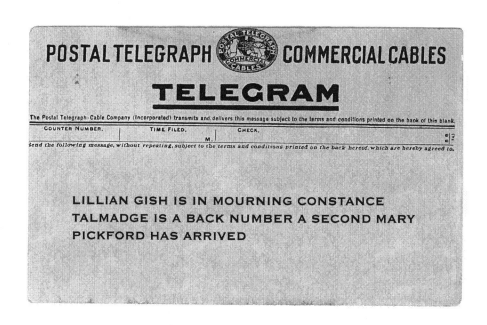

Assuming that Zelda had wanted a girl, Perkins writes to the new father,

66  If you are like me,…you will need some slight consolation and having
    had great experience with daughters—four of them, I can forecast that
    you will be satisfied later on."

※※※

#### Second.

In St. Paul, **Scott** has rented an office in town so he can get away from his
recuperating wife, the hired nurse, and the screaming baby. He's working on
a satiric play.

# ❧ NOVEMBER 18, 1921 ❧
## PARK THEATRE, COLUMBUS CIRCLE, NEW YORK CITY, NEW YORK

Let's hope things go better this time. Five days ago, social activist Margaret Sanger, 42, and her collaborator, former Liberal Member of the British Parliament Harold Cox, 62, showed up at Town Hall to give their scheduled talk, "Birth Control—Is It Moral?"

They were met by police, and one told them,

❝ There ain't gonna be no meeting. That's all I know."

*Margaret Sanger*

Sanger was arrested for disorderly conduct, but before the cops could take her away, she shouted,

❝ We have a right to hold [this meeting] under the Constitution...let them club us if they want to."

Of course she was released immediately, and the publicity is a godsend. Now they have a couple of thousand people lined up to hear her and Harold talk tonight about the taboo subject of—Shock! Horror!—birth control.

Sanger has been blocked out of many venues before. But this is the first time the interference has been so brutal. And, as far as she knows, the first time it has come on direct order from the Roman Catholic Archbishop of New York, Patrick J. Hayes, 54.

*Archbishop Hayes*

# 🎕 NOVEMBER 21, 1921 🎕
## GIRL SCOUT TEA HOUSE AT PEIRCE MILL, ROCK CREEK PARK, WASHINGTON, D. C.

O pening day at the tea house operated by the Girl Scouts of Washington, D. C., is going well.

This is the first time the public has visited the former restaurant, now redecorated with new curtains, furniture, and a fresh lick of paint, all in cheery blue and yellow. There was a nice write-up in the *Washington Post* yesterday, which is bringing in the crowds.

*Peirce Mill, Rock Creek Park*

The official grand opening was held two days ago for invited guests only, with the First Lady and honorary president of the national organization, Florence Harding, 61, doing the honors.

The specialty of the house is Florence's "Harding Waffles," made popular last year during her husband's presidential campaign. President Warren G. Harding, 56, loves waffles—smothered in chipped beef gravy [although the

Girl Scouts serve them with butter and syrup]—and Florence's recipe swept the nation. She is particularly careful to use ingredients which were rationed during the Great War, to underscore her husband's campaign theme of "Return to Normalcy."

# Florence Harding's Waffle Recipe

*Serves four*

**INGREDIENTS:**

   2 eggs
   2 tbls. sugar
   2 tbls. butter
   1 tsp. salt
   1 pt. milk
   Flour to make thin batter.
     (I use about 2 cups flour)
   2 large tsp. baking powder

**INSTRUCTIONS:**
- Separate the eggs.
- Beat yolks and add sugar and salt.
- Melt butter then add milk and flour and stir to combine.
- Beat egg whites until stiff (but not dry) peaks form.
- Stir one spoonful of whites into the mixture to lighten and then fold remainder of egg whites and baking powder.
- Bake in a hot waffle iron.

*From the* 1921 Atlanta Women's Club Cookbook

# ❧ NOVEMBER 24, 1921 ❧
## *LIFE* MAGAZINE, NEW YORK CITY, NEW YORK

A poem by free-lance writer **Dorothy Parker**, 28, is published in the humor magazine *Life,* edited by her Algonquin Hotel lunch friends, **Robert Benchley**, 32, and Robert Sherwood, 25. She praises the new hot Broadway star, Lynn Fontanne, 33, appearing as the ditzy title character in *Dulcy,* written by two of **Parker's** other lunch friends, **Marc Connelly**, 30, and **George S Kaufman**, 32, based on a character by another one of their friends, columnist **FPA [Franklin P. Adams]**, 40.

### "Lynn Fontanne"

#### By **Dorothy Parker**

"*Dulcy,* take our gratitude,
All your words are gold ones.
Mistress of the platitude,
Queen of all the old ones.
You, at last, are something new
'Neath the theatre's dome. I'd
Mention to the cosmos, you
Swing a wicked bromide."

# ❧ FALL, 1921 ❧
## BELLEVILLE, OUTSIDE OF PARIS

From his perch high atop the step ladder, American ex-pat Gerald Murphy, 33, can get a better view of the huge canvas he is working on, refurbishing the sets for the Ballets Russes.

*Serge Diaghilev*

Serge Diaghilev, 49, the founder and director of the ballet company, has asked Gerald, his wife Sara, just turned 38, and some other young students who are studying painting to travel out here daily to his atelier to restore the sets designed for his Ballet by local artists. Such as George Braque, 39, Andre Derain, 41, and Pablo Picasso, 40.

The Murphys jumped at the chance. Not only have they had the opportunity to meet some of the top cubist painters of the time, they get to hang out with the crowd around the Ballets Russes. Gerald is thrilled that they are not only allowed to watch rehearsals, they are *expected* to. And to discuss their opinions of the work.

These artists are not like the ones they have known before back home in America. Gerald sees Picasso as "a dark, powerful physical presence," like a bull in a Goya painting. And the Spaniard seems particularly interested in Sara.

Their life in Paris is so much different—so much better—than what they left behind when they boarded the *SS Cedric* for Southampton, England, in June.

Gerald has taken a leave of absence from the landscape architecture course he was enrolled in at Harvard. They packed up the kids—Honoria, three-and-a-half; Baoth, two; and Patrick, eight months—and the nanny and spent some time in England visiting the stately homes that Sara had known when she went to school there as a child.

*The Murphy family in America*

Didn't like it. Really hot summer and the gardens were all parched and brown.

They decided to go to Paris for a bit and then head home.

But when the Murphy family arrived here in early September, their American friends convinced them to stay. Everyone's coming to Paris.

After the Murphys had been in their furnished apartment at 2 rue Greuze for about a month, Gerald was stopped in his tracks by a display in the window of an art gallery: Cubist paintings, like the ones he had seen in the Armory Show in New York eight years ago, by some of the same artists—Braque, Derain, Picasso.

Gerald told Sara,

❝ That's the kind of painting that I would like to do."

He and Sara found a recently arrived Russian cubist/futurist, Natalia Goncharova, 40, who teaches painting in her studio on the rue de Seine in the Left Bank, and they have been taking lessons from her every day. Goncharova only allows abstract painting, nothing representational. Or, as Sara says,

❝ No apple on a dish."

Goncharova has created set designs for Diaghilev, so she told the Russian impresario about her eager American students and he immediately sensed an opportunity for free labor, getting his sets fixed up for the coming spring season.

*Natalia Goncharova*

The Murphys don't mind volunteering their services. They have Sara's family income of about $7,000 a year, and the franc is going for less than 20 cents on the dollar.

And in France, they can have cocktails with dinner. No Prohibition.

# ✁ BEFORE DECEMBER 3, 1921 ✁
## LIBRAIRE SIX, AVENUE DE LOWENDAL, PARIS

American ex-pat artist **Man Ray**, 31, is awfully chilly. He's been working inside this gallery with no heat, getting everything ready for his first solo exhibit here in Paris. **Ray** has been offered this show by French writer Philippe Soupault, 24, who recently opened this gallery inside his new bookshop, Librarie Six.

**Ray** and his friend, French artist Marcel Duchamp, 34, are planning a big party for the private viewing on the 3rd of December. They are hiding all the paintings by filling the room with balloons which they will pop all at once with their lit cigarettes, yelling Hurrah!

For the catalogue, **Ray** includes this biographical note:

    ❝   It's no longer known where Mr. **Ray** was born. After a career as a coal merchant, millionaire several times over and chair of a chewing gum trust, he has decided to accept the invitation of the Dadaists to show his latest canvases in Paris."

As **Ray** is working on hanging the exhibit, a little man, probably about 50 years old, looks at one of the paintings. **Ray** mentions to him that he is really cold. The man takes **Ray's** arm, and, speaking to him in English, leads him out on to the street to the local café, where he orders them both "hot grogs."

The man introduces himself to **Ray** as composer Erik Satie, 55, but starts speaking in French. **Ray** has to explain that he only speaks English. Satie says that it doesn't matter. And orders more grogs.

As they walk out of the cafe, the two men pass a shop displaying a bunch of household tools. **Ray** picks up a flat iron and motions Satie to follow him into the store. **Ray** uses Satie as a translator so he can buy glue and a box of tacks.

When he returns to the gallery,
**Ray** glues the tacks in a row to
the bottom of the iron. He wants
this to be a gift to his benefactor,
Soupault, so he adds it to the
exhibit and calls it *The Gift*.

*Erik Satie*

# ❧ DECEMBER 4, 1921 ❧
## CITY COURTHOUSE, SAN FRANCISCO, CALIFORNIA

Roscoe Arbuckle, 34, is awaiting the jury's verdict in his trial for manslaughter in the death of 26-year-old actress Virginia Rappe, after a drunken party in a hotel on Labor Day this year.

Arbuckle has protested his innocence since the day he was arrested. His attorney is optimistic about an acquittal.

The prosecutor, Matthew A. Brady, 46, has made this a show trial which will help his planned run for governor. He has used this as an opportunity to paint Roscoe, known to his fans as "Fatty," as a sexually depraved lecher. Just like all the other scum down in Hollywood.

However, Brady is not able to put his star prosecution witness, Maude Delmont, 35, a friend of the victim who was at the party, on the stand because there is evidence she has been trying to extort money from Arbuckle. Such as a telegram she sent to lawyers in San Diego:

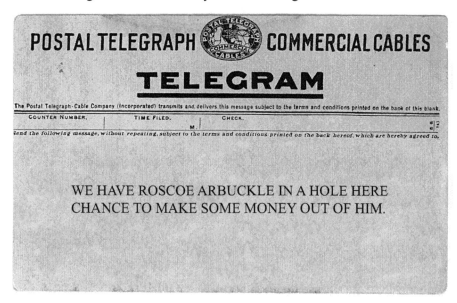

POSTAL TELEGRAPH COMMERCIAL CABLES

## TELEGRAM

The Postal Telegraph-Cable Company (Incorporated) transmits and delivers this message subject to the terms and conditions printed on the back of this blank.

| COUNTER NUMBER. | TIME FILED. | CHECK. | |
|---|---|---|---|
| | M. | | |

Send the following message, without repeating, subject to the terms and conditions printed on the back hereof, which are hereby agreed to.

WE HAVE ROSCOE ARBUCKLE IN A HOLE HERE
CHANCE TO MAKE SOME MONEY OUT OF HIM.

Of course, the whole story has been splashed over the front pages since the day it broke. Publisher William Randolph Hearst, 58, claims that this is selling more newspapers for him than the sinking of the *Lusitania* six years ago.

But even Roscoe's estranged wife, Minta Durfee, 32, has stood by him, showing up in court for support. Someone actually shot at her one day when she was coming to the courthouse!

Roscoe's co-workers have publicly stated that he could never have raped or murdered anyone. Charlie Chaplin, 32, whom he's known since their days at Keystone Pictures over seven years ago, told the papers that he "knew Roscoe to be a genial, easy-going type who would not harm a fly." Actor and director Buster Keaton, 26, issued a supportive statement also—and was promptly reprimanded by his studio.

But Arbuckle's films have been pulled from theatres and his reputation is shot.

And William S. Hart, about to turn 57, whom Arbuckle has never worked with or even met, said he thought "Fatty" was guilty.

Why can't they call him Roscoe?!

At the hospital, after examining Virginia, the doctor found no evidence of rape. At the hearing, the judge found no evidence of rape. The autopsy found there were no signs of violence on her body. The woman had a history of severe urinary infections, as well as getting quite drunk at parties, and curling up in pain.

Arbuckle's attorney had witnesses ready to testify to Virginia's sordid past. But Roscoe refused to let them. The poor woman is dead, for Chrissake.

At the end of the trial, last week, Arbuckle testified in his own defense. He remained surprisingly calm, and quietly answered each question put to him.

Now the jury is back.

Deadlock. 10-2 not guilty. They could not reach a unanimous decision.

The judge declares a mistrial.

# ❦ DECEMBER 7, 1921 ❦
## LA MAISON DES AMIS DES LIVRES,
## 7 RUE DE L'ODEON, PARIS

There's definitely a buzz. More than 200 people are crowding into two rooms in this small bookshop to hear French poet Valery Larbaud, 40, lecture and read from *Ulysses,* the latest work by Irish ex-patriate novelist James Joyce, 39.

This shop is owned by Adrienne Monnier, 29, whose partner, American ex-pat Sylvia Beach, 34, the owner of Shakespeare and Company across the street, is publishing *Ulysses* because no major publisher in America or England will touch it.

Publication date was supposed to be this autumn. But Joyce has been delayed by several bouts of bad health. His constant revisions are frustrating the printers. Those who have already subscribed to get the first copies are getting restless. They want *Ulysses!*

So Beach and Monnier have organized this reading to placate

LA MAISON DES AMIS DES LIVRES
*7, rue de l'Odéon, Paris - VI* — *Tél.: Fleurus 25-05*

*Mercredi 7 Décembre 1921*
*à 9 h. précises du soir*

SÉANCE CONSACRÉE A
L'ÉCRIVAIN IRLANDAIS

JAMES JOYCE
CONFÉRENCE PAR
M. VALERY LARBAUD

*Lecture de fragments de ULYSSES*
*traduits pour la 1re fois en français*

— *Nous tenons à prévenir le public que certaines des pages qu'on lira sont d'une hardiesse d'expression peu commune qui peut très légitimement choquer.—*

*Cette séance étant donnée au bénéfice de JAMES JOYCE, le droit d'admission sera, exceptionnellement, de 20 francs par personne. Nous serions particulièrement reconnaissants envers les personnes qui voudraient bien dépasser la somme fixée.*

*Les places doivent être retenues à l'avance. Nous rappelons qu'elles sont limitées à cent.*

*Invitation to* Ulysses *reading*
*[Photo courtesy of Glenn Johnston]*

impatient subscribers and promote the book among the French. At this point, they are hoping to bring it out on Joyce's 40th birthday, next 2nd of February.

Larbaud, who is not only a friend but a huge fan of Joyce, has been working for days in the back room of the shop with a bilingual Sorbonne music student, Jacques Benoist-Mechin, 20, to translate passages Larbaud can read to the crowd.

That's what's making Larbaud nervous. Although he has given talks here many times, never to a crowd this big. And never a reading with so much... well, sex in it.

In the invitation to the event, Beach and Monnier warn,

❝ Certain pages have an uncommon boldness of expression that might quite legitimately be shocking."

They don't mention that a New York City court has already found excerpts to be legally obscene.

Waiting in the dark room is American ex-pat artist **Man Ray**, 31, even though he doesn't understand much French. One American who is not here is the poet Ezra Pound, 36. He brought Joyce and his family to Paris over a year ago and promoted him and his work to all the right literati. Now he feels side-lined by the attention Beach's upcoming publication is getting.

Monnier gives Larbaud a glass of brandy to calm his nerves. On his way to the little table in front of the crowd, he steps behind the screen which is hiding Joyce from the audience to admit to the author that he is going to leave out a few lines.

Larbaud begins his talk by reviewing the life and previous writings of the Irish author. He links the novel *A Portrait of the Artist as a Young Man* and the short story collection *Dubliners* to this latest work and tells readers that the key to understanding Joyce's *Ulysses* is to keep Homer's *Odyssey* in mind.

Larbaud then reads translated parts of the "Sirens" and "Penelope" sections of *Ulysses* and is met with wild applause. At the end, Larbaud goes behind the screen and brings out Joyce, kissing him on both cheeks.

Joyce blushes.

# 🎗 DECEMBER, 1921 🎗

## RICHMOND, LONDON; LAUSANNE, SWITZERLAND; AND TAORMINA, SICILY

At the beginning of the month, the *London Times* reports that, because of an increase in

> " winter sickness...persons with weak hearts or chests must avoid rapid changes of temperature, which severely tax the circulation and which lower bodily resistance to infection."

The UK is on track for more than 36,000 deaths from influenza this year, mostly women.

In Richmond, southwest London, **Virginia Woolf**, 39, hangs up the phone after talking to the editor of the *Times Literary Supplement*. He wants her to change the word "lewd" in her review of Henry James' collection of short stories to "obscene." She says, fine.

She thinks, now that she has enough income from the Hogarth Press to spend her time writing novels, in the new year she won't have to compromise and write reviews anymore.

**Virginia** has been relatively healthy these past few months, but now she's feeling a bit of a cold and tiredness coming on.

*Hogarth House*

In Lausanne, Switzerland, T. S. Eliot, 33, recuperating from a nervous breakdown, has to tell his editor at *The Dial,* Scofield Thayer, just turned 32, that there will be another delay in his next "London Letter" for the magazine. There's no way it will appear until at least April, meaning a seven-month gap in columns.

Eliot blames it on a bad bout of the flu. He is using any energy he has right now to work on his long poem.

※❦※

In Taormino, Sicily, English ex-pat David Herbert Lawrence, 36, has sent off to his New York and London agents packets of revised short stories.

Now he's heading back to bed with an irritating case of the flu which won't go away.

Lawrence is, however, actually looking forward to spending Christmas sick in bed. He writes to a friend,

❝  I hate Christmas."

# ❧ MID-DECEMBER, 1921 ❧
## HOTEL SAINTE LUCE, AVENUE SAINTE-LUCE 1, LAUSANNE, SWITZERLAND; AND HOTEL PAS DE CALAIS, 59 RUE DES SAINTS-PERES, PARIS

Tom Eliot, 33, has a decision to make. His current plan is to leave Lausanne on Christmas Eve, when he should be done with the therapy treatments he is having here. He will go to Paris to join up with his wife, Vivien, also 33, who has been there on her own for the past few weeks.

Or he could stick around here for at least an extra week.

After he took a three-month leave of absence from his job at Lloyd's Bank, Tom and Viv spent some weeks at Margate, on the English coast, where Tom made great progress on his long poem.

After seeing the top nerve specialist in London, Eliot agreed with him that he needed to get away and rest.

One of their friends, Ottoline Morrell, 48, who had shared with them her own bouts of depression, recommended Dr. Roger Vittoz, 58, who had treated her brother here in Lausanne.

The Eliots went first to Paris, where Tom worked on the poem—really still a handful of fragments—with American ex-pat poet Ezra Pound, 36. Then Tom came here to begin treatments and Vivien stayed behind.

So far, Ottoline has been right about the town [although it's a bit dull], the food [which is excellent], the people [who are very helpful], and the doctor.

The Vittoz method includes the doctor holding Tom's head to read his brain waves and help to alter them. Vittoz gives Eliot exercises which involve repeating visuals and words which have brought him happiness.

Vittoz has been keeping Eliot busy, but he has found some times of calm to sit by Lake Geneva, working various moments he has experienced in to his epic.

The hotel is comfortable; the town is filled with chocolate shops, banks, and kids riding scooters over cobblestones.

From what Viv tells him, Paris is expensive. But any place in Europe is cheaper than London.

Tom is thinking he'll stay here until the new year.

Of course, he could also spend a few days on the Riviera…

*Ottoline Morrell*

In Paris, Vivien is not only worried about the expense, she is lonely. She has a little room high up in this hotel and can only afford to eat here instead of in any of the lovely Parisian cafes.

And when she's been out in the neighborhood, Vivien feels that any Brits she knows from back home have been avoiding her. Just the other day at the post office, art critic **Roger Fry**, just turned 55, was not happy to see her and made a hasty exit.

Paris is still cheaper than London. The Pounds have just moved into a lovely two-room studio around the corner for only £75 per year.

Maybe she and Tom should consider moving to Paris…

# ❧ DECEMBER 20, 1921 ❧
## HOTEL JACOB, 44 RUE JACOB, PARIS

The newlyweds, **Ernest**, 22, and Hadley **Hemingway**, 30, just arriving from Chicago, check in to the Hotel Jacob. The clerk hands them a note from fellow Chicagoan, Lewis Galantiere, 26, assistant to the American Commission to the International Chamber of Commerce, requesting that they meet him for dinner at Michaud's, a short walk away.

And so their new life begins.

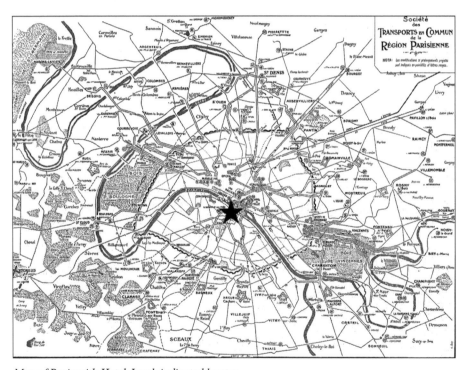

*Map of Paris with Hotel Jacob indicated by star*

# ❧ DECEMBER, 1921 ❧
## RICHMOND; AND WEST END, LONDON

In Richmond, the owners and operators of the Hogarth Press, **Virginia**, 39, and **Leonard Woolf**, 41, are quite pleased with the sales of their friend's book, *Twelve Original Woodcuts by Roger Fry,* just turned 55, which they hand-printed, bound and published themselves. The original press run sold out in two days!

Not the same for *Poems,* by their brother-in-law **Clive Bell**, 40. The art critic is thrilled that anyone wants to publish these 17 poems, written over the past 12 years, including "To Lopokova Dancing," an ode to the star of the Ballets Russes, Russian ballerina Lydia Lopokova, 30.

❧❧

In the West End of London, another one of the **Woolfs'** friends, economist **John Maynard Keynes**, 38, is returning to the Alhambra Theatre in Leicester Square. Since early November he has not missed a performance of the Ballets Russes' *The Sleeping Princess* with Lopokova as Aurora.

The production itself has gotten terrible reviews; one calling it a "gorgeous calamity." And **Keynes'** friends in Bloomsbury, once so enamored of the ballet company for its avant-garde

*Lydia Lopokova*

choices, have been turned off by this traditional re-staging of a three-act ballet from the end of the last century. They have even soured on Lopokova.

Serge Diaghilev, 49, impresario of the Ballets Russes, is losing his shirt on this one. After a disastrous first night he was seen to break down in tears. He received a huge advance against box office income from the Alhambra Company to mount this spectacle. Hardly anyone is coming and it has to run the full three months.

But none of this bothers **Maynard**. He's not coming back for the Tchaikovsky score, re-orchestrated by Igor Stravinsky, 39. Or the outlandish sets and costumes.

He returns every evening because he finds himself, much to his surprise and that of all his friends, absolutely entranced by Lydia.

*To see Lydia Lopokova dancing a few years before, go to https://www.youtube.com/ watch?v=BfIHu7b8J4k&fbclid=IwAR3u_4zsWC25sVavS6nO9byBJEc l97T795LcQjddIcuJxyVMHtZ72E9jf-Y*

# ❦ DECEMBER 27, 1921 ❧
## SCRIBNER'S, 153-157 FIFTH AVENUE, NEW YORK CITY, NEW YORK

The communication between editor Maxwell Perkins, 37, and his hit novelist, **F. Scott Fitzgerald**, 25, has continued as publication of **Scott's** second novel, *The Beautiful and Damned,* draws closer.

Last month Perkins wrote to **Fitzgerald** about a passage in which one of the characters makes disparaging remarks about the Bible. Max wasn't offended, but Scribner's has never published such heresy.

Max told **Scott** that he is concerned that some readers will believe **Fitzgerald** feels that way, writing,

*Maxwell Perkins*

❝ I think I know exactly what you mean to express…but I don't think it will go. Even when people are altogether wrong, you cannot but respect those who speak with such passionate sincerity."

**Fitzgerald**, working from a rented office in St. Paul, Minnesota, to avoid his wife and newborn daughter at home, took offense, replying:

❝ If this particular incident was without any literary merit…I should defer to your judgment without question. But that passage belongs beautifully to that scene."

That statement worried Perkins. He wrote back,

" Don't ever *defer* to my judgment. You won't on any vital point, I know, and I should be ashamed if it were possible to have made you, for a writer of any account must speak solely for himself."

**Fitzgerald** agreed to compromise. A little. He changed "Godalmighty" to "deity," cut "bawdy," and edited "Oh, Christ" to "Oh, my God."

But now **Fitzgerald** has sent Perkins a whole new ending, which his wife Zelda, 21, hates. **Scott** has cabled Max to get his opinion:

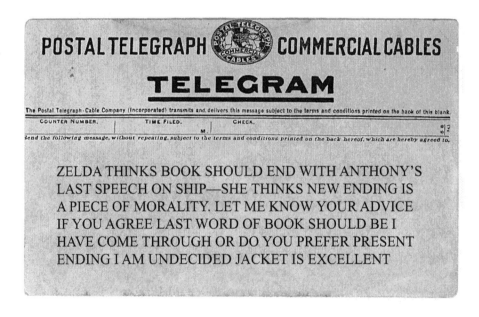

**POSTAL TELEGRAPH** **COMMERCIAL CABLES**

**TELEGRAM**

The Postal Telegraph-Cable Company (Incorporated) transmits and delivers this message subject to the terms and conditions printed on the back of this blank.

| COUNTER NUMBER. | TIME FILED. | CHECK. |
| --- | --- | --- |
| | M. | |

Send the following message, without repeating, subject to the terms and conditions printed on the back hereof, which are hereby agreed to.

ZELDA THINKS BOOK SHOULD END WITH ANTHONY'S LAST SPEECH ON SHIP—SHE THINKS NEW ENDING IS A PIECE OF MORALITY. LET ME KNOW YOUR ADVICE IF YOU AGREE LAST WORD OF BOOK SHOULD BE I HAVE COME THROUGH OR DO YOU PREFER PRESENT ENDING I AM UNDECIDED JACKET IS EXCELLENT

So today Perkins cables him,

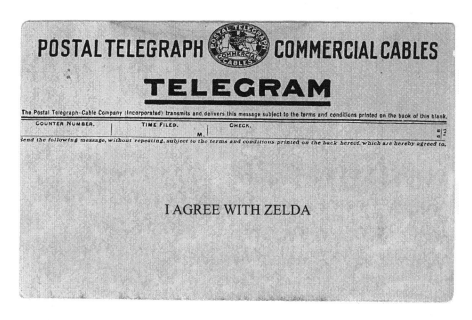

and then sits down to write a more detailed explanation in a follow-up letter:

> 66 I think she is dead right about that…[The intended satire] will not of itself be understood by the great simple-minded public without a little help. For instance, in talking to one man about the book I received the comment that Anthony was unscathed; that he came through with his millions and thinking well of himself. This man completely missed the extraordinarily effective irony of the last few paragraphs."

Perkins sends off the letter and edits the copy for the dust jacket so as to underline the irony.

# ❧ DECEMBER 31, 1921/ ❧
# JANUARY 1, 1922
## IRELAND, ENGLAND, FRANCE AND AMERICA

At the end of the second year of the 1920s…

In Ireland, at Dublin's Abbey Theatre, still directed by one of its founders, **Lady Augusta Gregory**, 69, the company is finishing up the run of a double bill including *A Pot of Broth* by one of its other founders, Irish poet **William Butler Yeats**, 56. The Abbey has been performing this little one act about gullible peasants since it was written over 15 years ago.

*Newspaper headline, December 8*

Throughout the country, violent atrocities are being committed by the Irish Republican Army and the British Black and Tans. In Dublin, in a huge leap forward for Irish independence, the government of the Irish Free State is finally coming into being.

❧❧❧

In England, near Oxford, **Yeats** is encouraged by the news of the signing of the Anglo-Irish Treaty, giving Ireland, including 26 of the island's 32 counties, Dominion status in the British Commonwealth. He writes to a friend that he expects the Irish parliament, the Dail, will ratify the treaty, but

  ❝  I see no hope of escape from bitterness, and the extreme party may carry the country."

With the establishment of the Irish Free State, **Yeats** and his wife Georgie, 29, are thinking of moving back to Dublin in the new year with their two children, Anne, two, and the recently christened Michael Butler Yeats, four months old.

In Sussex, **Virginia**, 39, and **Leonard Woolf**, 41, have come to their country home, Monk's House, for the holidays.

The Hogarth Press, the publishing company they have operated out of their home in the Richmond section of London for the past four years, is steadily growing. In total they published six titles this year, a 50% increase over last.

A book of woodcuts by a friend of theirs, **Roger Fry**, 55, that they brought out just a few months ago is going in to its third printing.

Their assistant, Ralph Partridge, 27, was at first helpful. Now he works in the basement, sleeps over during the week and has a bad habit of leaving the press and metal type dirty, which drives **Leonard** crazy. Partridge's profit-sharing deal has increased from last year but is only £125.

Before they came down here to ring in the new year, the **Woolfs** had a visit from their friend, one of their former best-selling writers, Katherine Mansfield, 33. They discussed excerpts from a new work, *Ulysses,* by Irish novelist James Joyce, 39, to be published in Paris early in the new

*Katherine Mansfield*

year. Mansfield agrees that it is disgusting, but she still found some scenes that she feels will one day be deemed important.

About three years ago, **Virginia** and **Leonard** were approached about publishing *Ulysses,* but they rejected it. They don't regret their decision.

In France, Paris has become home to over 6,000 Americans, enjoying being let out of the prison of Prohibition back home.

Writer **Gertrude Stein**, 47, who has lived here for almost 20 years, has been laid up recently after minor surgery. She is still writing, working on *Didn't Nelly & Lilly Love You,* which includes references to her birthplace, Allegheny, Pennsylvania, and that of her partner for the past 14 years, **Alice B. Toklas**, 44, San Francisco, California, and how the two of them met in Paris.

Because she recently visited the nearby studio of another American ex-pat, painter and photographer **Man Ray**, 31, who just moved here last summer, **Gertrude** works in to the piece "a description of Mr. **Man Ray**."

*The author at Gertrude Stein's house in Allegheny, Pennsylvania*

In America, New York free-lance writer **Dorothy Parker**, 28, is attending, as usual, the New Year's Eve party hosted by two of her friends from lunches at the Algonquin Hotel—*New York World* columnist **Heywood Broun**, 33, and his wife, journalist Ruth Hale, 34. Their party is an annual event, but bigger than ever this year because it is being held in their newly purchased brownstone at 333 West 85th Street.

**Parker** notes that they are directly across the street from one of the buildings that she lived in with her father.

**Dottie** is here alone. Her friends don't expect her husband, stockbroker and war veteran Eddie Pond Parker III, 28, to be

*Building across the street from the Brouns' brownstone*

with her. They joke that she keeps him in a broom closet back home.

She's enjoying talking to one of her other lunch buddies, top *New York World* columnist **Franklin Pierce Adams** [always known as **FPA**], 40, who is professing his undying love for **Parker**. While sitting next to his wife and keeping an eye on a pretty young actress in a pink dress.

All the furniture except for some folding chairs has been removed to make room for the 200 guests and a huge vat of Orange Blossoms [equal parts gin and orange juice, with powdered sugar thrown in]. No food or music. Just illegal booze.

As the turn of the new year approaches, the guests join the hosts in one of their favorite traditions. **Dottie** and the others each stand on a chair.

At the stroke of midnight they jump off, into the unknown of 1922.

*Thanks to Neil Weatherall, author of the play,* The Passion of the Playboy Riots, *for help in unravelling Irish history.*

# TO READ...

Quentin Bell. *Virginia Stephen, 1882-1912,* and *Mrs. Woolf, 1912-1941.* Vols. I and II of his *Virginia Woolf: A Biography.* London: Hogarth Press, 1972. His uncle Leonard Woolf asked him to write it and he did a great job.

A. Scott Berg. *Max Perkins: Editor of Genius.* New York: E. P. Dutton, 1978. The full excellent biography, by the Pulitzer-prize winning *Lindbergh* and Katharine Hepburn biographer.

Kevin Birmingham. *The Most Dangerous Book: The Battle for James Joyce's* Ulysses. New York: The Penguin Press, 2014. Detailed look at the struggle to get *Ulysses* published. God bless Sylvia Beach.

Michael Cunningham. *The Hours.* New York: Farrar, Straus and Giroux, 1998. A well-deserved Pulitzer went to this creative and fascinating novel that, like *Mrs. Dalloway,* weaves three stories in different time periods together. Woolf's original title for her novel was *The Hours.*

Kathleen Dixon Donnelly. *Manager as Muse: Maxwell Perkins' Work with F. Scott Fitzgerald, Ernest Hemingway, and Thomas Wolfe.* Birmingham, UK: K. Donnelly Communications, 2014. 'Nuff said.

Kathleen Dixon Donnelly. *"Such Friends": The Literary 1920s, Volume I—1920.* Pittsburgh, PA: K. Donnelly Communications, 2021. A collection of my blogs about what was happening 100 years ago in 1920. First in a series.

Noel Riley Fitch. *Sylvia Beach and the Lost Generation: A History of Literary Paris in the Twenties and Thirties.* New York: W. W. Norton and Co., 1983. A detailed and fascinating look at this amazing woman and her friendships with the other characters in Paris at the time.

Kevin Fitzpatrick. *The Dorothy Parker Society.* His excellent website [https://dorothyparker.com/book-shop] includes books by and about Parker and the Round Table. All of his are good, along with the Facebook group and his walking tours in Manhattan. Highly recommended.

Brendan Gill. *Here at* The New Yorker. New York: Random House, 1975. The semi-official biography of the magazine up until the 70s.

Bill Goldstein. *The World Broke in Two: Virginia Woolf, T. S. Eliot, D. H. Lawrence, E. M. Forster and the Year that Changed Literature.* New York: Henry Holt and Company, 2017. Centered mostly in London, he does a good job of connecting these four separate lives.

Arlen J. Hansen. *Expatriate Paris: A Cultural and Literary Guide to Paris of the 1920s.* New York: Arcade Publishing, 2012. In an almanac format organized by areas of the city, this chronicles who was there and where they lived. Good to take with you when you go.

Joseph M. Hassett. *The* Ulysses *Trials: Beauty and Truth Meet the Law.* Dublin: Lilliput Press, 2016. He brings a lawyer's point of view to both trials. And he really doesn't like John Quinn.

Ernest Hemingway. *A Moveable Feast.* New York: Charles Scribner's Sons, 1964. His version of events, as he remembered them years later.

Kevin Jackson. *Constellation of Genius: 1922: Modernism Year One.* London: Hutchinson, 2012. A month by month listing of what was happening in this important year for literature. Good as a reference but no pictures!

Brenda Maddox. *George's Ghosts: A New Life of W. B. Yeats.* London: Picador, 1999. Focuses on his late-life marriage and is a really good read.

Marion Meade. *Bobbed Hair and Bathtub Gin: Writers Running Wild in the Twenties, Edna St. Vincent Millay, Dorothy Parker, Zelda Fitzgerald, and Edna Ferber.* New York: Harcourt, Inc., 2004. Meade does well expanding her Parker research to include the other fabulous women.

Marion Meade. *Dorothy Parker: What Fresh Hell Is This?* London: Heinemann, 1988. The best. Excellent biography and the basis for the film, *Mrs. Parker and the Vicious Circle* as well as the A&E *Biography* program.

James R. Mellow. *Charmed Circle: Gertrude Stein and Company.* New York: Avon Books, 1974. The best overall book about this era and the characters in Paris.

Emily Midorikawa and Emma Claire Sweeney. *A Secret Sisterhood.* London: Aurum Press, 2017. A terrific look at the literary friendships of Austen, Bronte, Eliot and Woolf by two great friends of mine in the UK.

They also run a fascinating website on female literary friendships, www. SomethingRhymed.wordpress.com.

Ulick O'Connor. *Celtic Dawn: A Portrait of the Irish Literary Renaissance.* London: Black Swan, 1984. The best history of the whole time period and the characters involved.

B. L. Reid. *The Man from New York: John Quinn and His Friends.* New York: Oxford University Press, 1968. Read it if you must, but it's a slog and it makes this absolutely fascinating man seem boring.

Michael Reynolds. *Hemingway: The Paris Years.* Cambridge, MA: Basil Blackwell, 1989. Just one part of the best multi-volume biography and also one of the most detailed accounts of Paris at the time.

Diane Souhami. *Gertrude and Alice.* New York: Pandora, 1991. Better than a biography of either one of them, the author writes about both equally and, most interesting, about their relationship.

Frances Spalding. *Vanessa Bell.* London: Weidenfield and Nicolson, 1983. In writing about Roger Fry she discovered Vanessa Bell and wrote this definitive biography. I'm including this one of her books, because it's my favorite. But anything by her is great.

Gertrude Stein. *The Autobiography of Alice B. Toklas.* New York: Vintage Books, 1990. If you've ever been afraid to read Stein, this is the place to start. Definitely her point of view, and a wonderful romp.

Colm Toibin. *Lady Gregory's Toothbrush.* London: Picador, 2003. The title comes from her comment after the *Playboy* riots, "It's the old battle between those who use a toothbrush and those who don't." By the Irish author of the novel *Brooklyn*.

Colm Toibin. *Mad, Bad, Dangerous to Know: The Fathers of Wilde, Yeats and Joyce.* London: Penguin, 2018. Terrific book about three amazing Irishmen—and their sons.

W. B. Yeats. *Selected Poetry.* Ed. with an introduction and notes by A. Norman Jeffares, London: Macmillan, 1990. The best collection of his best poems; the introduction is a good overall mini-biography.

# TO WATCH...

*Albert Nobbs.* [2011] Glenn Close, Janet McTeer. There aren't really any feature films about the Irish Literary Renaissance—and neither is this one. But it is a beautiful evocation of Dublin in the late 19th century. A long time labor of love for Close, it netted her and McTeer Oscar nominations.

*Carrington.* [1995] Jonathan Pryce, Emma Thompson. Excellent film about the relationship between Lytton Strachey and his partner, Dora Carrington. The beginning scenes show the Bloomsbury group at Vanessa Bell's Sussex house, Charleston, where it was filmed.

*Genius.* [2016] Colin Firth, Jude Law, Laura Linney. Max Perkins editing a novel doesn't sound like much of a basis for a film, but Firth's Perkins and Law's bombastic Tom Wolfe strike just the right note. Linney as Perkins' wife is the only American actor as a main character, and all filming was done in the UK. Go figure.

*The Hours.* [2002] Nicole Kidman, Julianne Moore, Meryl Streep. Award-winning film version of Michael Cunningham's book (see above). The scenes of Los Angeles in the 1950s were all filmed where we lived in Hollywood, Florida.

*Midnight in Paris.* [2011] Owen Wilson, Kathy Bates. Directed by Woody Allen, who is in love with the city and the time period. "I am Dali!"

*Mrs. Dalloway.* [1997] Vanessa Redgrave, Natascha McElhone. Directed by Marleen Gorris, Redgrave was a great choice to portray Virginia's favorite heroine.

*Mrs. Parker and the Vicious Circle.* [1994] Jennifer Jason Leigh, Scott Campbell, Matthew Broderick. Excellent film based on Meade's biography of Parker (see above). It has the look and feel of the time and the characters. Yes, she did mumble like that, so you might want to have the rewind button handy. There are numerous clips on YouTube.

*Paris Was a Woman.* [1996] This terrific documentary focuses on the female relationships in Paris in the 1920s, with a lot about Sylvia Beach's support of James Joyce.

*The Ten-Year Lunch.* [1987] Good documentary about the whole Algonquin group, narrated by Heywood Broun's son, CBS sportscaster Heywood Hale Broun. Includes interviews with Marc Connelly, Helen Hayes, Ruth Gordon, and Averell Harriman, among others. A bit outdated, but they're all dead anyway.

# To visit...

*The Abbey Theatre.* [https://www.abbeytheatre.ie/]. On Abbey Street in Dublin, the theatre came up with a creative schedule for a COVID19 2020 season, so there is a lot you can experience on line at their site and on Facebook. They also have a detailed archive of all their productions.

*The Algonquin Hotel.* [https://www.algonquinhotel.com/]. At 59 West 44th Street, the hotel has been refurbished many times and each new owner has pledged to retain its literary history. The latest Algonquin cat, Hamlet, has his own Facebook page, but hasn't been very active lately.

*BloggingWoolf.* [https://bloggingwoolf.wordpress.com/]. Run by Paula Maggio of Kent State University, this is one of the best blogs to follow for all things Woolfian.

*Charleston Farmhouse.* [https://www.charleston.org.uk/]. On your next European trip—Go. You'll have to drive or take a taxi from nearby Lewes, but it is well worth it, particularly during their May festival.

*Coole Park.* [https://www.coolepark.ie/]. Lady Gregory's home about 35km south of Galway city, near Gort, is now a national park, without the house but with the autograph tree. Well worth a visit next time you are driving around the west of Ireland.

*The Dorothy Parker Society.* [https://www.facebook.com/groups/dorothyparkersociety]. This Facebook group is run by Kevin Fitzpatrick and you can find all of his terrific books there. When you're planning to go to New York again, check out his walking tours. For 20 years he has been keeping the flame with events and publications. Highly recommended.

*The Dublin Literary Pub Crawl.* [https://www.dublinpubcrawl.com/]. My main Dublin tip, particularly for your first night there. Two actors lead a group of tourists around the main part of the city, stopping to do scenes from Irish literature and theatre, punctuated by drinks in pubs. Great way to get the lay of the land. Until it's safe to travel again, you can buy their book from the site.

*Monk's House.* [https://www.nationaltrust.org.uk/monks-house]. Virginia and Leonard's country home is part of the National Trust, well worth a visit, and not far from Charleston.

*The National Library of Ireland* [www.nli.ie]. The Library has the best exhibit about Yeats and all his "Such Friends," and I've seen a lot of them. You can access it online and, eventually, in person. Great gift shop—and, ladies, use the downstairs restroom. Trust me.

*Philomena Mason.* [philomenamason.wordpress.com] is an Irish playwright and a friend of mine. She has written plays on Lady Gregory and her husband, Sir William, as well as other Irish characters from history, which have been performed in Ireland and the UK. They are delightful. Excerpts are up on her new website, and she will be adding info in the future.

*Shakespeare and Company.* [https://www.facebook.com/groups/131979076789] Until it's safe to travel again, you can join their Facebook group. The real shop is on a totally different site, directly across from Notre Dame, but worth a visit. Then go sit in one of the cafes. They are still there.

*Sissinghurst.* [https://www.nationaltrust.org.uk/sissinghurst-castle-garden] Vita Sackville-West's home is known especially for its gorgeous gardens. If you can, stay at the B&B on the grounds.

*"Such Friends."* [Suchfriends.wordpress.com]. On the blog I am currently chronicling The Literary 1920s. Hopefully, there will be eight more books.

*"Such Friends." Virginia Woolf and Bloomsbury Group* [www.voicemap. me]. My own walking tour of the area is available to download for your mobile or computer.

*Thoor Ballylee.* [https://yeatsthoorballylee.org/home/], Yeats' tower, "with the river on the first floor," as Ezra Pound said, is near Coole Park, and also worth the trip when it is open again. They often sponsor events in the summer around his June birthday.

# ABOUT THE AUTHOR

*Kathleen Dixon Donnelly, Ph.D.*

Kathleen Dixon Donnelly has been involved in teaching and the creative process for more than 40 years. Her thesis for her MBA from Duquesne University in her hometown of Pittsburgh, Pennsylvania, was *Manager as Muse: Maxwell Perkins' Work with F. Scott Fitzgerald, Ernest Hemingway and Thomas Wolfe,* available on Amazon in both print and e-book versions.

*"Such Friends": The Literary 1920s* is based in part on her dissertation for her Ph.D. in Communications from Dublin City University, on the creative development of writers in early 20th century salons.

She has led walking and driving tours of Dublin and Coole Park in Ireland; London and Sussex in England; and the Left Bank of Paris. You can walk with her through Bloomsbury by downloading her tour, *"Such Friends": Virginia Woolf and the Bloomsbury Group* from www.voicemap.me. She has given numerous presentations about the writers throughout the United Kingdom at the Southbank Centre, the University of the Third Age, and in the United States at the English Speaking Union, and Osher Lifelong Learning programs.

Kathleen has self-published a series of books from her blogs as *Gypsy Teacher,* chronicling her voyages on Semester at Sea and relocation to the United Kingdom, available on Amazon.

She recently retired as a senior lecturer in both the School of Media and Business School at Birmingham [UK] City University. She lives with her Irish husband Tony Dixon and their two cats, Gertrude Stein and Robert Benchley, in Pittsburgh.

You can contact her by email at kaydee@gypsyteacher.com, through Twitter @SuchFriends, or through her blog, www.suchfriends.wordpress.com.

Made in the USA
Middletown, DE
22 September 2021